The Future of Blasphemy

Also available from Continuum

Does God Hate Women? Jeremy Stangroom and Ophelia Benson
Humour and Religion Walter Van Herck and Hans Geybels
War and Ethics Nicholas Fotion

The Future of Blasphemy

Speaking of the Sacred in an Age of Human Rights

Austin Dacey

continuum

Continuum International Publishing Group

The Tower Building	80 Maiden Lane
11 York Road	Suite 704
London SE1 7NX	New York NY 10038

www.continuumbooks.com

British Library Cataloguing-in-Publication Data
A catalogue record for this book is available from the British Library.

ISBN: HB: 978-1-4411-0737-4
       PB: 978-1-4411-8392-7

Library of Congress Cataloging-in-Publication Data
Dacey, Austin, 1972-
The future of blasphemy : speaking of the sacred in an age of human rights / Austin Dacey.
    p.   cm.
Includes index.
1. Freedom of speech – Religious aspects. 2. Blasphemy. I. Title.
BL65.B54D33 2011
364.1'88–dc23

                                                                                    2011020978

Typeset by Newgen Imaging Systems Pvt Ltd, Chennai, India
Printed and bound in India

Contents

Preface

Eighty years ago, an extraordinary collection of short fiction in Urdu was published in India under the title *Angarey* (Embers). The contributors were condemned in the local press for blasphemy for their searing commentaries on contemporary Muslim society. Local clerics called for the authors' deaths by stoning. One of them was a young gynecologist named Rashid Jahan whose writings "Dilli Ki Sair" (Sightseeing Trip to Delhi) and "Parde ke Peeche" (Behind the Veil) spoke of women's experience of isolation and concealment in the practice of *purdah*. She was branded *Angareywali*—The *Angarey* Woman—and threatened with having acid thrown in her face and her nose cut off. In March 1933, the British colonial government began to confiscate and destroy the book under Article 295-A of the Indian Penal Code, which criminalized works made with the "deliberate and malicious intention of outraging the religious feelings of any class of His Majesty's subjects." Only five copies survived.

I came upon the story of the *Angarey* affair while finishing this book and found that it conveyed my themes more compellingly than I could hope to do. First, the contemporary talk of blasphemy in the international public square is neither a recent invention nor a return of a medieval theological specter. Rather, it is a distinctly modern phenomenon in which blasphemy has been reframed within the secular idiom of respect for persons. Second, this principle of equal respect, forged in European liberal political thought and foundational to a just and open society, is all too easily appropriated in the service of illiberal and patriarchal notions of identity, propriety, and "honor." Third, those most vulnerable to the abuse of laws against blasphemy and therefore most vocal in defiance of them are dissidents within the very communities whose "feelings" the laws are purportedly protecting. Finally, such dissidents are not just engaging in "free speech" but manifesting religiously heterodox or secular commitments of conscience that are no less worthy than those they affront.

My first exposure to these matters came only in 2000 with the imprisonment for blasphemy of Younus Shaikh, a medical professor in Islamabad. While completing my graduate studies in applied ethics and social philosophy, I had taken a position with the Center for Inquiry, a secularist think-tank in upstate New York that joined with other members of the International Humanist and Ethical Union to bring greater awareness to Dr. Shaikh's case. The Center's founder, the philosopher Paul Kurtz—who also published a translation of *Lajja* (Shame), the 1993 novel by Taslima Nasrin that provoked charges of outraging religious feelings under Bangladesh's Article 295-A—supported me in becoming the organization's first representative to the United Nations several years later. It was in this capacity that I participated in the debates surrounding freedom of expression and "combating defamation of religions" at the Human Rights Council in Geneva in 2008 and 2009.

It was my good fortune to receive personal introductions to the Council and its highly politicized internal workings by Diane Ala'i, Hossam Bahgat, John Fisher, Roy Brown, and David Littman, along with my colleague Hugo Estrella. There I also met with Tarek Fatah, Walid Phares, and Naser Khader. The Center for Inquiry supported visits to the Netherlands and Denmark, which helped me to locate these debates within the wider European conversation on freedom and secularism. Nicole Esteje conceived of and organized dialogues in the Netherlands with Maurits Berger, Coskun Çörü, Rabbi Raphael Evers, Martijn de Koning, and Nahed Selim; I learned much from talks with the Danish philosopher and journalist Malene Busk. On an earlier trip to South Asia, I received personal introductions to the religion and politics of the region from Vikas Gora, Shahriar Kabir, Innaiah Narisetti, Santishree Pandit, and Goparaju Vijayam. I also consulted with Zinda Bajwa, a representative of the Ahmadiyya Muslim Community in New York City.

In developing the ideas of this book, I benefited additionally from exchanges with Paul Berman, Paul Cliteur, Evan Derkacz, Angela Evenhuis, Peter Foges, Tariq Ismail, Melik Kaylan, Marie Korpe, J. K. Miles, Alva Noë, Ole Reitov, Rob Tielman, Raquel Saraswati,

Nathan Schneider, Floris van den Berg, Michael Weiss, Bob Worth, and Banafsheh Zand-Bonazzi. Drafts were read by Ophelia Benson, Afshin Ellian, Patrick Hopkins, Arif Humayun, Tariq Ismail, Barry Kosmin, Stephen Law, Angela McAllister, and David Nash. Nash's excellent history stressed the modern (post-seventeenth-century) nature of what I call personal blasphemy as well as its continuity with European norms prohibiting hate speech. The work of Hossam Bahgat and the Cairo Institute for Human Rights Studies influenced me to approach the issue from within the framework of promoting equality. The International Humanist and Ethical Union's Roy Brown and Matt Cherry pointed the way to analyzing the problem as one of discrimination against secularists and heterodox believers. Meanwhile, my reading of Winnifred Fallers Sullivan and others along with conversation with Colin Koproske had convinced me that the legitimate rights of traditional religious believers must be subsumed under more general rights belonging to all. Hubert Dreyfus and Sean Dorrance Kelly's book *All Things Shining* emboldened me to speak of the secular engagement with the sacred.

Individual pieces were refined by editors at *Free Inquiry*, *Trouw*, and *Religion Dispatches* (with permission from the latter, some material is reprinted in Chapters 1 and 5), by audiences at various universities where I spoke, and by my students in human rights at Marymount Manhattan College. When I decided to put something more lasting on paper, Ophelia Benson and Jeremy Stangroom recommended Continuum. What began as a briefing on the UN debates—which changed dramatically in March 2011, when the backers of the defamation resolution abandoned that language in exchange for "incitement to imminent violence," the standard for criminalization favored by the United States—morphed at the suggestion of the publisher into a monograph for the religious studies list. This gave me the luxury of being less timely. The result is an idiosyncratic mix of historical and legal analysis with admittedly speculative philosophical reflection. Along with Continuum's editors, Philip Dacey read it all and saved me from many embarrassments. Throughout, it was the encouragement of Angela McAllister that fortified me to write and her patient attention that graced me at every stage. The sins of omission and commission are all mine.

Despite the outcry of zealots and the colonial laws that came to their aid, Rashid Jahan and her colleagues sparked a new movement in Urdu literature, inspiring writers such as Ismat Chughtai, who kept the censors busy in her own day. It is to their embers, still shining, that I dedicate my own modest offering.

Berkeley, California
October 2011

1 Combating the defamation of religions

And none knows its interpretation, save only God.

—*Quran, Surah Al-Imran 3:7*

"History shows that criminalizing speech doesn't work," the representative of the United States was saying when the chairman cut her off. We were gathered in a windowless conference room beneath the Palais des Nations, the sprawling home of the United Nations Human Rights Council in Geneva, Switzerland. The Organisation of Islamic Cooperation, or OIC, was our host for an "open-ended informal consultation" on a draft resolution it planned to introduce at the Council later that month, March 2009, entitled "Combating defamation of religions." I was sitting in on the negotiations on behalf of a New York-based secularist think-tank, one of the many civil society groups lobbying the UN in an effort to combat the OIC's agenda.

At the close of the session, late in the afternoon, I had struck up a conversation with Marghoob Saleem Butt, a member of the permanent mission of Pakistan to the UN, who was chairing the meeting on behalf of the OIC, a 57-member intergovernmental organization that presented itself as "the collective voice of the Islamic world."[1] We soon were joined by members of the US, Canadian, and European Union delegations, all of whom had roundly criticized the resolution's language, starting with its title. The Pakistani diplomat met his Western critics with kindly eyes and a smile worn thin with impatience. It was what in UN circles would be called a dialogue among civilizations. But, of course, civilizations do not talk to each other—only people do.

The text of the draft resolution, which dozens of country delegations had spent hours dissecting, began with a preamble noting "with deep concern the instances of intolerance, discrimination and acts of violence against followers of certain faiths" and "the negative projection of certain religions in the media and the introduction and

enforcement of laws and administrative measures that specifically discriminate against and target persons with certain ethnic and religious
backgrounds, particularly Muslim minorities following the events of
11 September 2001."[2] Stressing "the need to effectively combat defamation of all religions and incitement to religious hatred in general
and against Islam and Muslims in particular," the resolution stated
that the Human Rights Council

> Deplores the use of the print, audio-visual and electronic media, including
> the Internet, and any other means to incite acts of violence, xenophobia
> or related intolerance and discrimination towards any religion, as well as
> targeting of religious symbols and venerated persons; . . .
>
> Strongly condemns all manifestations and acts of racism, racial discrimi-
> nation, xenophobia and related intolerance against national or ethnic,
> religious and linguistic minorities and migrants and the stereotypes often
> applied to them, including on the basis of religion or belief, and urges all
> States to apply and, where required, reinforce existing laws when such xen-
> ophobic or intolerant acts, manifestations or expressions occur, in order to
> deny impunity for those who commit such acts; . . .
>
> Urges all States to provide, within their respective legal and constitutional
> systems, adequate protection against acts of hatred, discrimination, intimi-
> dation and coercion resulting from defamation of religions, and incitement
> to religious hatred in general, and to take all possible measures to promote
> tolerance and respect for all religions and beliefs; . . .

Since 1999, the OIC had been bringing such resolutions to the United
Nations, first at the Human Rights Council and later at the General
Assembly, and passing them easily, thanks to a broad coalition with
Russia, China, Cuba, and the "non-aligned movement" of developing
countries. They were celebrating a decade of combating defamation
of religions.

"What if," the chairman asked us, "someone were to say that the
Virgin Mary was not a virgin but a promiscuous woman?" Surely there
could be no point to this but defamation. The Canadian representative
observed that "defamation" has a specific legal meaning—entailing the

spread of falsehoods that harm the livelihood of some individual—that is not applicable to cases of religiously offensive speech. For starters, religious personages like the Virgin Mary and the Prophet Muhammad are not, legally speaking, alive, so they are not persons before the law who can be harmed.

Never mind, I thought, how one would demonstrate, in a court of law, the falsity of a scurrilous rumour about a far-distant and long-departed religious figure. Sadly, it seems all the world's blasphemers could never do more damage to the reputations of gods, saints, and prophets than has already been done by their devoted followers. The odd thing about God is that no matter how much he is slandered, his livelihood never suffers as a result. I did not bring this up. Undeterred by Canada's logic, Chairman Butt pointed out that this is precisely why the authorities must be called upon to defend holy figures against insult: they are not around to defend themselves.

Though I was peering at the scene through the glass of blasphemy, the biblical, Greco-Hebraic concept of a direct verbal affront to the divine has no precise equivalent in Islamic tradition, which has been more concerned with idolatry and fidelity to doctrinal truth. Blasphemy is typically compared to *takdhib*, literally "giving the lie, denial" and *iftira* or "invention." Both are infractions of the truth, one the denial of religious truth, the other the assertion of falsehood.[3] In English-language international fora, Pakistani and other OIC diplomats and their supporters deployed the ostensibly non-theological concepts of "respect," "insult," and "defamation." Even the World Union of Muslim Scholars used the secular term *isa'ah*—denoting insult, harm, or offence.[4]

In the context of the unique social relationship between Muslims and the Prophet Muhammad, however, "insult" had special significance. According to the traditional understanding, while Muhammad was a prophet, tribal leader, war chief, and moral arbiter, he was not divine. He was a human being whose honor had to be protected by public expressions of loyalty and esteem.[5] In traditional Islamic law, insulting the Prophet or Allah was the crime of *sabb*. Committed by Muslims, it constituted *ridda*, or apostasy, a repudiation of the faith.

Committed by non-Muslims, it violated the terms of their status as *dhimmis*, tolerated and protected second-class subjects of the Islamic state.[6]

The chairman and we, his Northern audience both talked about "defamation." We assumed our meanings were shared. But the concept of respect at stake was not the equal dignity of the citizen, at home in modern European political thought, but the exceptional honor reserved for a historically singular individual, irreplaceable in the moral and social order of a community. Divided by a common language, we could only nod.

After years of abstaining from the votes on the OIC's anti-defamation resolutions, European democracies were now leading a push against the very concept—flanked by the US, which had recently rejoined the politically contentious Human Rights Council under the newly installed Obama administration. Their objection was fundamental: persons have rights; religions do not. As the EU put it, "human rights law protects primarily individuals in the exercise of their freedom of religion or belief, rather than the religions as such."[7] Freedom of belief protects the person who believes or disbelieves, not the content of the belief. The charge of the Human Rights Council, as the heart of the system of international human rights law, is to protect and promote the principles set out in the 1948 Universal Declaration of Human Rights. That Declaration, which heralds "a common standard of achievement for all peoples and all nations," exists to safeguard the fundamental freedoms of individuals, among them the freedom of expression, guaranteed by Article 19, and the freedom of religion and conscience, including the freedom to doubt and dissent, guaranteed by Article 18. Blasphemy, it would seem, is a human right.

In the wake of the Muhammad cartoon crisis, many European intellectuals and policy makers were anxious to affirm the freedom of speech vis-à-vis Islam, to assert a "right to blasphemy" at the heart European democratic tradition, as *Die Welt* had put it.[8] And yet, a number of these democracies criminalized blasphemy, while almost all of them criminalized "hatred," "insult," or "defamation" of the religious. European human rights courts had generally upheld such laws, finding that they did not violate international guarantees of freedom of expression and conscience. The Organisation of Islamic Cooperation decried what it saw as a vicious double-standard. The Europeans, it seemed, would cleave to free speech about Muhammad, just not about Jesus or the Jews. When Chairman Butt was pressed during the consultation, he invoked *Ross v. Canada*—a case in which an international body vindicated a Canadian Supreme Court decision for "protecting the 'rights or reputations' of persons of Jewish faith"—and asked, "Why can't we extend this protection to *all* religions?"[9] In July 2009, Ireland appeared to do just that, by passing a bill criminalizing expression "grossly abusive or insulting in relation to matters held sacred by any religion." That October, in the proceedings of a committee chaired by Algeria, the OIC attempted to insert the anti-defamation standard into the Convention on the Elimination of All Forms of Racial Discrimination, which is, unlike the resolutions, an enforceable treaty. The Pakistani delegation, speaking on behalf of the OIC, proposed the adoption of language borrowed, chapter and verse, from the Irish law.[10]

The OIC's campaign against defamation of religions could be seen as a cynical political maneuver. The controversy elevated the stature of the OIC, giving it a platform on which to present itself as the self-appointed emissary of the *umma*. It also furnished diplomats with weapons in the rhetorical battles over human rights violations in international fora. Hoisting the language of respect and tolerance as a shield, states with deplorable human rights records such as Pakistan, Iran, Egypt, Sudan, China, Cuba, and Venezuela could lodge accusations of rampant violations on European and US soil in a grand *tu quoque*.

In Pakistan, the defamation of religion was already a crime.[11] The Penal Code provided for imprisonment and capital punishment for blasphemy, a fact that invaded international consciousness with the assassination of Salman Taseer, the Punjab province governor, and Shahbaz Bhatti, the country's only Christian cabinet member, both of whom opposed the blasphemy laws. According to the National Commission for Justice and Peace, nearly 900 people had been charged since their introduction. Still others had been harassed or killed by vigilantes while authorities stood by. The laws were used most often to persecute the nation's religious minorities, Christians and the Ahmadiyya Muslim community, a sect numbering between 3 and 4 million who are officially deemed apostates because they dissent from Sunni orthodoxy.

As the delegates in Geneva were retiring for an evening of fine dining, four Ahmadi teenage boys sat in prison in Pakistan, confined to a single cell for twenty-four hours a day and denied proper medical care. Muhammad Irfan, Tahir Imran, Tahir Mehmood, and Naseer Ahmad had been accused of desecrating the Prophet by writing his name on the bathroom wall of a mosque in Punjab province. Although no evidence was presented, the head of the local police felt that "the gravity of the case against Islam justified arresting the children first."[12] Local religious extremists had made it clear that they would avenge the insult if the authorities would not. Others have been even less fortunate. In September 2009, a 19-year-old Christian named Fanish Masih was accused of flushing a chapter of the Quran down a drain and held in solitary confinement. He was found dead in his cell. The warden said Masih hung himself. Others called it "extra-judicial murder."[13]

Pakistan's hypocrisy was virtuosic. Even as it appeased the most hate-filled elements in its society, it spouted self-righteous lectures at Western democracies on the stereotyping of minorities and the need to promote diversity. While the resolutions by the General Assembly and Human Rights Council were non-binding, they carried the moral imprimatur of the United Nations. They served to legitimize the suppression of peaceful religious heterodoxy and political dissent elsewhere in the world—first and foremost in dozens of self-described Islamic states where blasphemy and "public order" are used by authoritarian governments to control public speech and opinion.

At the head of the empty UN conference room, the US representative began to explain to the chairman why her country would continue to fight the OIC's entire approach, but he was looking away, reading an email on his smart phone. Apparently he was unaware that he was exemplifying the Americans' solution to the problem of speech that offends: Ignore it, and if that does not do, start your own conversation.

The debate over the defamation of religions cannot be separated from a global political movement to "Islamize" human rights standards. In 1981, OIC states produced a Universal Islamic Declaration of Human Rights. While the document, like its 1990 successor, the Cairo Declaration on Human Rights in Islam, lifts a phrase or two from the Universal Declaration of Human Rights, its novel contribution is to constrain the universal standards by subordinating them to religious law. The Cairo Declaration states, "All the rights and freedoms stipulated in this Declaration are subject to the Islamic Shari'ah." Where the Universal Declaration affirms freedom of expression, the Cairo Declaration suggests that it is Islam, and not the individual believer or disbeliever, that deserves protection: "Everyone shall have the right to express his opinion freely in such manner as would not be contrary to the principles of the Shari'ah." In 2007, the Pakistani Ambassador to the UN told the Human Rights Council on behalf of the OIC that the Cairo Declaration "is not an alternative, competing worldview on human rights. It complements the Universal Declaration as it addresses religious and cultural specificity of the Muslim countries."[14] For some, it seems that universality is not enough.

The Islamic human rights movement was particularly disturbing in light of the flouting of universal standards by OIC countries and the lack of a robust regional human rights regime of monitoring and enforcement in the Middle East and North Africa. The fiercest resistance had come from civil society activists within those countries who were documenting violations and pressing their governments and international bodies for reform. In April 1999, representatives of one hundred nongovernmental organizations convened in Casablanca for the First International Conference of the Arab Human Rights Movement: "Prospects for the Future."[15] Convened by the Cairo Institute for Human Rights Studies, the conference yielded a declaration of its own, the Casablanca Declaration, which asserted that international human rights law and the United Nations instruments and declarations are "the only source of reference" for human rights, rejecting "any attempt to use civilisational or religious specificity to contest the universality of human rights."[16]

Despite its claims to represent Muslim interests, the OIC appeared to represent the interests of autocrat and ambassadorial corps above all else. Human rights groups such as the Cairo Institute were among the most vocal critics of the OIC's agenda at the United Nations. They knew what was said in Geneva and New York would reverberate in Cairo and Damascus. At the same time, advocates of free speech in the Arab world had a hard time finding allies in Europe.[17] For the far Right, it was 1683, and the shadow of the Crescent was falling across the gates of Vienna.[18] The struggle over religious defamation was a battle in the war to preserve Judaeo-Christian civilization from the insidious "Islamization" of the continent. Meanwhile, many on the Left found their better angels at war with one another. They wanted to defend an Enlightenment culture of irony, satire, anti-clericalism, anti-authoritarianism, and critical reason in public life. And yet in solidarity with the marginalized, they were drawn to the ostensible rationale of the OIC's campaign.[19] The surprising fact is that, years before Pakistan had introduced its resolutions combating the defamation of religions, the European Court of Human Rights in Strasbourg had already invented and enshrined in human rights law a "right to respect for religious feelings."

Idioms of blasphemy

"Respect" works for diplomats for the same reason that it makes work for philosophers: it is multiply, prodigiously ambiguous. You can respect the force of the sea, experiencing awe and deference toward a power greater than yourself that is both humbling and uplifting. You can respect a person's talents or achievements, appreciating the merits of a work or a trait of character. You can respect a person's honor or standing in a social community. And you can respect a person by recognizing his equal standing in the moral community, as an agent with the authority to hold you accountable to him, no less than you can hold him accountable to yourself. The first respect can be called *respect as reverence*, the second *respect as appraisal*, the third *respect as honor*, and the fourth *respect as recognition*.[20] The object of this last kind of respect is not excellence, merit, or fearsome power, but rather *authority*. It is not an evaluation of worth, but instead a commitment to entering into a mutual relationship with another in which the claims of each can have the status of reasons to the other.[21]

Something like the first two forms of respect can be found in the attitude toward a just law. We defer to its power and judge it to be sound or right. In monotheistic thinking, reverence, appraisal, and a kind of recognition respect are united in the attitude toward a divine lawgiver that is also a person. In the person of a sovereign god, the seat of moral authority is at once an awesome power, the paradigm of the true, right, and good, and an agent who can make claims on us, and on whom—in some way—we can make claims. A defining moment in the history of Western thought and political culture was the assertion that these three kinds of respect could also be met in the human, mortal person. We can appraise persons' virtues and works, and judge some more worthy than others. But fundamentally we recognize persons as equal authorities—those to whom we are answerable and who are answerable to us. This authority is to be revered as the source of "human dignity." The idea of respect for equal standing came as a radical challenge to the idea of respect for honor, rooted in the pre-modern aristocratic order of European life and arrayed around nobility, rank, and esteem as signs of social status. Where honor had buttressed a hierarchical social structure, respect would found an egalitarian form of moral and political community.

Though it had many antecedents, the idea began to emerge in the twelfth-century Christian discourse of natural law. It was Immanuel Kant who elevated respect, *Achtung,* to the status of the ultimate moral principle. The autonomy of the person, he thought, is the source of the moral law, and so in submitting to the law we are at the same time recognizing the "inalienable dignity" of the mutually accountable other, exalted "above any price," which stirs reverence—*reverentia*—in us.[22] Liberal thought bequeathed a picture of the person as intrinsically, incomparably valuable and inviolable. That picture was set at the heart of the ideology of human rights, described by the 1789 Declaration of the Rights of Man and of the Citizen as "sacred."

The contemporary quandary over blasphemy does not begin in Danish cartoons, or Satanic Verses, or even in the UN convention in 1966 banning "religious hatred." It begins in 1617 with the creation of the English common law offence of blasphemous libel. Across Europe, secular authorities were inventing a secular rationale for the centuries-old religious crime, adapting it to the new, modern conception of the state as a compact among persons for the protection of their rights. In this conception of the state, the moral premises for the law were supplied by respect for individual citizens. And so, what the common law of blasphemy instituted was not a crime against one's maker, but a crime against one's neighbor, the crime of outraging the sensibilities of the religious. Blasphemy had become personal.

If the language of universal human rights did not exist, it would have to be invented. But it is the wrong language in which to talk about blasphemy. In the civil and political arena, the language of human rights is designed to defend the individual from the arbitrary power of states. Its conceptual tools are respect for persons and injury to persons, and so it naturally analyzes the problem of blasphemy as a problem of interpersonal disrespect and injury. As law, this is illegitimate and discriminatory. As culture, it is impoverished.

Blasphemy laws may be *de jure* or *de facto*—they may single out a particular traditional religious community or a family of communities for protection from blasphemy as such, or they may attempt to limit blasphemous expression through more general legal instruments regulating the defamatory, the offensive, the indecent, the insulting or the hateful. Consistent with the international guarantees of freedom of expression, freedom of conscience, and equality before the law, there is a strong prima facie case against banning blasphemy *de jure*. In a pluralistic society that embraces unbelievers and religious dissenters, *de jure* blasphemy laws constitute a failure of equality before the law, for they fail to provide comparable protection of the consciences of the secular and heterodox. *De facto* blasphemy laws empower judicial elites—or vocal groups of citizens—to bar some viewpoints from public discourse. However, in a democracy, a free and open public discourse is a condition of the legitimacy of the state.

While the quasi-secular laws of personal blasphemy perpetuated the inequality of their more theological forebears, they introduced new potential for illiberal abuse, for they took as their standard for wrongdoing the subjective feelings of the aggrieved. And because they were ostensibly motivated by the liberal principle of equal respect for persons, they could permanently lodge themselves in the legal systems of liberal democracies, this despite the fact that no one has demonstrated that the criminalization of religious defamation and hatred actually brings about a world with less ignorance, bigotry, and malice.

Culturally, by using the language of universal human rights to understand the act of blasphemy, we run the risk of losing other useful and important ways of talking about it. The hegemony of human rights discourse in legal and political spheres can influence broader cultural conversations in much the same way that the hegemony of market economies and commercial culture can influence thinking about love, art, food, or living things. If we allowed the liberal discourse of legal injury to individuals to become the preeminent culturally respectable and authoritative way of talking about blasphemy, we would have diminished our conversations about what may or may not be sacred, and how one should respond to it. Talk of respect for persons crowds out other objects of reverence, and the din of the categories of "religious insult," "religious defamation," and "religious hatred" deadens our ears to the possible desecration of secular values.

The language of defamation, incitement, provocation, denigration, dishonor, offence, insult, and hatred trains attention on the respect of recognition. The machinery of liberal rights is first and foremost a machinery designed for upholding this one form of respect. In the system of liberal rights, reverence is reserved for the very same entity that deserves recognition—the dignity of the human person. The language of abomination, defilement, desecration, profanation, violation, transgression, and sacrilege invokes the respect of appraisal and the respect of reverence. And it does not foreclose the possibility that proper objects of these attitudes can be found outside of the individual person. To imagine that the modern legal discourse captures everything there is to care about is to assume from the outset that the claims of reverence beyond persons are false, or that their truth could be ignored. The idea of reverence for the moral authority of the sacred, and evaluation of the claims made on its behalf, are lost in the anxious rush to ensure recognition of the moral standing of the person.

There are many important questions of sacredness that simply cannot be grappled with from inside the cramped space of the liberal discourse of respect for persons and individual rights. Are the lives of animals sacred, or merely valuable? Does nature awe us because it is sublimely holy, as Emerson thought; because it is monstrously evil, as Schopenhauer thought; or because it is majestically tragic, as Darwin thought? Which taboos are prejudices, and which mark an inviolable boundary—miscegenation, transgenomics, androgyny, homosexuality, incest, bestiality, necrophilia, cannibalism? Which boundary-crossings are merely comminglings and which are abominations?[23] What is it that may not be laughed at?

Other languages are available to us. Experimental psychology and anthropology can speak of social boundaries, purity and pollution, and the set apart. Literature and art offer still other idioms, of integrity and identity, fetish and attachment, showing and not showing, naming and remaining silent. If I am lucky, Anglo-American moral philosophy can have something to offer as well. And of course, religious traditions are a rich resource of idioms on sacrilege. In a later chapter, I attempt to illustrate this by appropriating some of the pluripotent notions of idolatry found in medieval Islam.

None of this is to deny that the language of universal human rights is the best language in which to discuss state interference in peaceful expressions of sacrilege. While the doctrine of individual rights is not the appropriate frame for the claims of the accusers, it is the appropriate frame for those accused of blasphemy who face coercion of their conscience and expression. The accused must be protected by universal norms of freedom of conscience and expression, but the accusers should have no case unless their rights have been violated. To focus on anything but personal rights in the sphere of law would be unjust. To focus on nothing but personal rights in the sphere of culture would be blind.

The future of blasphemy

The book begins with a brief swoop over the history of the European experience with criminalizing blasphemy. This survey in Chapter 2 is motivated primarily by three assumptions. First, European legal discourse is integral to the international debate on blasphemy and human rights. The legal traditions of European states have influenced traditions around the world through the legacy of colonial governments, and they continue to exert a degree of moral influence in global politics. Further, the supranational human rights regime of Europe is the most advanced of all of the regional human rights regimes in the world. The judgments made within this regime therefore have unique power as legal precedent. Second, the ethical traditions with which I engage emerge in late-medieval and early-modern European thought. The history situates these legal and ethical discourses within the development of liberal democracy in the West. Finally, the history reveals that the contemporary debate is heir to a number of different conceptions of blasphemy corresponding to different concepts of reason and respect.

Chapter 3 presents a moral analysis of the forms of concern, respect, and recognition that persons extend to each other by granting each other equal standing in a moral community. It makes the case that treating a person with equal concern and respect can be consistent with offending his sensibilities, and in some cases presents a positive reason to do so. Further, sacrilege can contribute to the civic virtue of avoiding appeals to authority and force in public life, and instead seeking and offering reasons for our commitments wherever possible. Chapter 4 presents a case against all laws prohibiting blasphemy, "defamation of religions," and "advocacy of religious hatred" on the grounds that such laws require the state to select among contested beliefs about the sacred and contested understandings of citizens' religious and ethnic identities. In doing so, the state interferes with the formation of public opinion in an open public discourse and thereby undermines the democratic legitimacy of its authority. Finally, Chapter 5 presents a spiritual-philosophical case that an openness to sacrilege is a safeguard against investing the wrong things with sacredness. In Abrahamic traditions, this is the sin of idolatry. But even secular people can engage in the struggle to know and respond appropriately to the sacred, understood as the domain of objectively vital, inviolable, and incommensurable values. Their blasphemy can be wanton, but it can also be an affirmation that, for them, the genuinely sacred lies elsewhere.

Although I hope that these contributions constitute an advance, I am afraid that they do not always make an advance by making things better. Many of these questions do not admit of easy or happy answers, so we should be skeptical of melioristic solutions. In some places, our options run from bad to awful. Where conflict and loss seem inevitable, we can only try to clarify what is at stake and who, if anyone, is responsible. While my analysis does not assure agreement, and in some cases proceeds by excavating deeper disagreements, it does suggest a basic moral grammar—of concern, respect, recognition, insult, accountability, blame, autonomy, authority, and legitimacy—that can be shared even by those across a divide of desecration. It also uncovers symmetries between the position of the desecrator and the position of the venerator.

These debates typically are framed as clashes between the secular and the sacred, between freedom and devotion. Such frames trivialize both blasphemy and belief. From a legal perspective, blasphemy is often best analyzed as not only as an exercise of freedom of expression but also as an exercise of freedom of religion or conscience. When the Ahmadiyya employ the *azan*, or call to prayer—thereby blaspheming against conservative Sunni belief—they do so as part of their spiritual practice. We miss something important if we think of this as "free speech." We could also analyze the intolerant religious practices of the conservative Sunni as "expressions" that blaspheme what is sacred to the Ahmadi. The same rights and duties shape the space of personal liberty of thought and expression in which both belief and disbelief move. I will argue that the symmetry extends not just to dissenting religious practitioners but to secular persons of conscience as well. Sacrilege by seculars can be seen, no less than can a religious practice, as an assertion about what is and what is not genuinely sacred. The same principles that lead us to recognize the value of the religious practice should also lead us to recognize the value of the sacrilege.

The future, we can hope, belongs not to personal blasphemy but to ethical blasphemy, ethical in two senses. First, it is primarily a matter of moral and civic responsibilities, not of legal rights and obligations. Second, it is a category and a concern belonging not just to members of traditional religions, but to any person of conscience who would speak of the sacred. Now, legally speaking, this would first require the defeat and the end of blasphemy, religious defamation, and religious hatred as *crimes*. The space for ethical blasphemy in culture is best protected by eliminating the crime of personal blasphemy from law. Western democracies have a moral imperative to end their criminalization of blasphemy and religious hatred not just because it is illegitimate. Within the new international covenant of universal human rights, the legal choices of liberal democracies have consequences for the struggle for fundamental freedoms in illiberal regimes elsewhere. These crimes keep us talking about offence, affront, insult, and intolerance—talking about ourselves. What we should be talking about is where sacredness can be found. To talk about that, we have to be free to talk about where it cannot be found.

2 Sacrilege

Therefore, behold, I am against the prophets, saith the Lord, that steal my words every one from his neighbor.

—*The Book of Jeremiah 23:30*

We do not know what the first blasphemer said. We do know that he was a stranger who came among the Israelites. Leviticus 24, the primordial text on the primordial trial for this crime in the Western tradition, tells us that the stranger "blasphemed the Name, and cursed," but it does not tell us the words he used. Not sure exactly what punishment was appropriate for this stranger, whose father was an Egyptian, the Israelites took the man into custody and waited to hear what God willed to be done.

> And the Lord said to Moses, Bring out of the camp him who cursed; and let all who heard him lay their hands upon his head, and let all the congregation stone him. And say to the people of Israel, Whoever curses his God shall bear his sin. He who blasphemes the name of the Lord shall be put to death; all the congregation shall stone him; the foreigner as well as the native when he blasphemes the Name shall be put to death.[1]

Under Mosaic law, blasphemy was a direct verbal offence against the God. In the biblical Hebrew, the Leviticus text uses the words *nakob*, literally to enunciate or pronounce distinctly, and *qillel*, meaning to curse, with connotations of piercing, railing, repudiating, disrespecting, denouncing, insulting, and abusing.[2] To restate the utterance would have been to repeat the insult, and to invite fresh wrath from heaven. In the later practice of Jewish law, even the witnesses at a trial for blasphemy were prohibited from recounting the offending words until the sentencing phase, when all observers were removed from the chambers. The judges would then hear the repetition of the blasphemy, stand and rend their own garments in grief, never to mend them.

The Greek translation of the Hebrew text, the Septuagint, renders the verbs *nakob* and *qillel* with *blasphemein*, which takes its roots from "to hurt" and "to speak." *Blasphemein*, to hurt by speaking, was opposed with *euphemein*, a more common Greek term useful in religious contexts. Euphemy, etymologically, "speaking well," was the uttering of only apt words when performing sacred rites, which could mean uttering nothing at all, and instead keeping a holy silence.[3]

A holy silence was, of course, at the heart of the first Abrahamic faith. Not even Abraham, who spoke with God personally, knew his name. God revealed himself to Abraham in Exodus 6 only as *El Shaddai*, or God Almighty. Throughout the Bible and Talmud, God is known under many divine epithets: *Elohim*—God, *El Olom*—God Everlasting, *El Khai*—The Living God, *El Elyon*—God Most High, *Abir*—The Strong, *Kedosh Yisroel*—Holy One of Israel, *Tzur Yisroel*—Rock of Israel, Melekh—The Ruler, *Adonay Tzivaot*—Lord of Hosts, *Adonai*—Lord. The true name of God, the *Shem Hameforash*, or sacred Name, though it can be written in The Tetragrammaton of the Hebrew letters Yud, Hay, Vav, and Hay—transliterated as YHWH or YHVH, is too sacred to be vocalized.[4] The traditionally observant would pronounce the Name aloud by saying *Adonai*.

The scope of this chapter is blasphemy in the narrow Greco-Hebraic sense as well as sacrilegious acts more broadly. Since sacrilegious acts are typically directed against representations or icons of the divine or sacred, they typically have an expressive dimension, if only implicitly. Iconoclasm and desecration communicate something about what an icon or a grave represent. I will often use "sacrilege" and "blasphemy" interchangeably, except where I want to refer to the biblical model or to a prohibition on "blasphemy" as such.

The history of sacrilege and the law is entangled with the history of normative authority. What counts as a reason for action? When do you defer to something in your thinking about what to feel and do? What has regulatory power over the country of your wants, impulses, fears, and intentions? These are questions of normative authority. Questions of normative authority are bound up with the problem of political legitimacy, the moral justification of the use of coercive force on the members of a community. In the history of the legal regulation of blasphemy in the West, three broad phases emerge: an ancient conception of blasphemy as a direct verbal affront to the divine; a medieval conception of a seditious challenge to the sanctity of law, the public order or common good; and finally a modern notion of an offence against the sensibilities, rights, or dignity of individual religious believers.[5] These conceptions of blasphemy correspond roughly to three models of authority: the biblical model with God as the source of normativity, a medieval model of authority in the hands of a divinely sanctioned ecclesiastical or temporal ruler, and the modern model in which the individual person is the ultimate source of normativity.

Spiritual

The oldest and most far-reaching argument for the legal prohibition of blasphemy assumes that one of the legitimate purposes of government is to prevent direct insult to the divine. Here the Mosaic law is paradigmatic. What is contrary to God's will is a sin; what is a sin is a crime; so the proscription of abusing the Name is inescapable. There is a certain austere majesty to the Mosaic model, set in high relief against the desert skies. Yet it immediately looks less attractive if any of the following conditions fail to obtain: there is clearly one god, whose intentions are clear; this god intervenes in the world; and strangers are rare. In the subsequent evolution of the societies of Judeo-Christian heritage, lawmakers and citizens found that each of these assumptions came under severe pressure.

To consider the divine-intervention condition first: For centuries, the fear of direct divine retribution was for elites and ordinary people alike a powerful justification for criminalizing blasphemy.[6] It might have turned out that we lived in a world in which God avenged the abuse of his name by providential intervention, calling down flood or famine or plague, turning black the tongue of the blasphemer. The reality of a thin-skinned and short-tempered deity participating in world events would have been sufficient grounds for a public policy banning blasphemy. However, with the passage of time and the growth of human knowledge, the providential worldview grew less, not more, plausible. In any event, what divine punishment there might be has not proven swift, unequivocal, or certain enough to serve as an effective deterrent.

Instead, the retribution was to come from secular power. But how was blasphemy to be punished? If it really were, as St. Thomas Aquinas argued in his 1265–74 *Summa Theologica*, a sin more grave than murder, how could anything less than death even approach proportionality between crime and punishment?[7] God was the most important entity in the world, and one could neither rob, nor maim, nor kill him. The worst thing that could be done to the most important entity in the world was to desecrate the Name. No human crime could compare with the desecrating of the most sacred name. Yet even a human murder could merit the ultimate sanction. So, the legal regimes that proliferated across Europe dealt death for the egregious blasphemy or repeat offender, often preceded by sentences of public humiliation and disgrace, the slicing of lips, the removal of lips, and the piercing and severing of the tongue.[8] The punishments of shame and ridicule "focused both the opprobrium and laughter of the community upon the convicted individual" and "made communal opinion stronger than miscreants and their words."[9] The mutilation of the mouth is a symbolic approximation to the existential gravity of the sin—a disfigurement of one's very person by amputation of the voice.

The profanation by the stranger of Leviticus could have been a slip in judgment, a malapropism riding on a burst of enthusiasm. Most victims of Europe's earlier blasphemy laws were not eloquent, spiritually motivated heretics, but common people who were caught in a momentary lapse of discipline or decorum. The tavern and the gambling hall were hotbeds in the medieval and early modern policing of speech as drink and boisterous conviviality loosened tongues.[10] And everywhere in the margins of medieval life were the permanent miscreants, the cretinous, the stricken, the insane, who through lack of cognizance or care could not be parties to the covenant. The Omnipresent One must hear every one of these indignities, but could the magistrate smite them all on his behalf? If only a smattering were to be smitten, how could enforcement avoid arbitrariness, and how could the punishment maintain its overawing aura of a sacral restoration of transcendent balance? The more common this garden-variety profanity, the more it called into question the tenability of civil prosecution for sacrilege.

The last person to be executed for blasphemy in Great Britain was a 20-year-old sometime student at the University of Edinburgh named Thomas Aikenhead, who fell prey to the moral panic of local Presbyterian ministers of the Privy Council and was hanged on 8 January 1697 for railing against God and the Trinity.[11] The Aikenhead affair shocked the conscience of generations of European thinkers. If death seemed to be the only sentence proportionate to the crime of blasphemy, understood as the profanation of the sacred, it also stood out as grossly disproportionate as against the other sanctions of the criminal law. If the wrongness of blasphemy is its abuse of the divine Name, then its evil is unsurpassed, and no sentence would be too harsh. If, however, it is to be treated within a general system of positive law, it will inevitably be compared to other crimes of thought and speech similar in form and found its punishment to be unreasonably, or—so it seemed to many horrified observers of the Aikenhead execution—sadistically, excessive.[12]

The appalling excesses of punishment could perhaps have been stomached if—contrary to conditions of the Mosaic scene—the interloping of strangers into the midst of the covenant people had been rare and exceptional, the occasional foreigner of Egyptian extraction wiped out in a spasm of divine violence. Instead, when the guardians of the descendents of Hebrew religion moved in from the deserts, up from the cellars and catacombs, eventually to take over cities, kingdoms, and empires, they found themselves overseeing worlds full of strangers. The condition of the unitary and univocal God, convenient to theocrats, was no less precarious even in the Sinai scenario. The Mosaic achievement fundamentally was the triumph of the one god over the many gods of polytheistic practice. What Moses could not have been prepared for was how the People of the Covenant would become a People of the Book. With the coming of the Word came the end of the holy silence around the Name. What began as a word from a mountaintop, became an avalanche of words, from the Septuagint to the Latin Vulgate Bible to the scriptoria of the monastic orders. Texts do not read themselves, and in countless individual readings by countless individual persons, apocrypha, ambiguity, and mistranslation invited constructive and creative reinterpretation. The text would be both a font of spiritual innovation and an alternative epistemic authority that could be held higher than the authority of Rome.[13]

Out of the desert, in this teeming intellectual environment, the condition of the univocal and unequivocal God—the first, monotheistic condition of the Mosaic world—was increasingly difficult to sustain. Christian leaders had long been forced to contend with the presence of the Jews, who had lived in the midst of their communities in a condition of second-class citizenship with its origins in the fourth-century laws of Constantine.[14] The Fourth Lateran Council, convened by Pope Innocent II in Rome in November 1215, concerned itself with Jews marrying Christians, Jews holding public office, and Jews whose very appearance in public on Good Friday could be taken as an affront by Christians in mourning: "we forbid most severely, that any one should presume at all to break forth in insult to the Redeemer. . . . we command that such impudent fellows be checked by the secular princes by imposing on them proper punishment so that they shall not at all presume to blaspheme Him who was crucified for us."[15]

A dualistic counter-tradition had also haunted Christianity since its rise to temporal power under the Roman empire, when it was forced to compete with the expansionist Manichean religion—inspired by Mani, a third-century Syriac Aramaic speaker from Persian Babylonia. The Manicheans believed that the material world was not created by God but by an evil deity who had imprisoned them in flesh. Their ideas were disseminated among literate Christians by the writings of the Church Father, St. Augustine of Hippo—an adherent in his youth—and other anti-Manichean polemical texts.[16]

The eleventh and twelfth centuries also saw the spread of fresh religious fervor among lay clerics and believers and with it the spread of new Christian counter-traditions and dissident practices. The distinction between heresy and blasphemy is not always clear in medieval thought, but heresy typically involved the adoption of heterodox belief on the basis of some principled theological or philosophical grounds. Blasphemy, on the other hand, could be a sacrilegious word uttered without any theological intent or counter-belief. Heresy embraced a lie, while blasphemy mocked a truth. The term *heresy* comes from the Greek *haireisthai*, to choose. Robert Grosseteste made recalcitrance in belief a necessary condition for heresy, which he defined as "an opinion chosen by human perception, contrary to holy scripture, publicly avowed and obstinately defended."[17]

Early in the twelfth century, Christian leaders and thinkers became fixated on heresy. In its early initial life, the charge of blasphemy was often an adjunct, a kind of aggravating factor, in the prosecution of heresy. The first major European law against blasphemy had appeared with the Town Ordinances and Privileges of Vienna in 1221.[18] Emperor Frederick II and Louis IX followed suit, and by the late fourteenth century, the public infliction of blasphemy sentences was a spectacle common to the medieval city and town across the continent. With Reformation and Counter-Reformation came new waves of anti-blasphemy statutes struggling to contain the explosions of doctrinal diversity. In 1209 the Church launched a military campaign, the Albigensian Crusade, against a heretical sect that had become entrenched in the French province of Languedoc, the Cathars. While the Cathars considered themselves Christians, as a consequence of their Manichean-like dualistic metaphysics many believed that Christ had not become flesh but only inhabited it. Therefore, they adopted heterodox stances on the significance of the crucifixion and the reality of Holy Communion. In the wake of the Crusade, the Inquisition continued the grizzly work of excising the errant words from the tongue. One of the accused was Béatrice de Planissoles.

We do not know just what Béatrice said. She came to the attention of the Inquisition in 1320 because of a report that she had made blasphemous remarks about the Eucharist, the sacrament of Holy Communion. Her Inquisitor was Jacques Fournier, Bishop of Pamiers, who would later go on to become Pope Benedict XII. Fournier had made it his mission to stamp out the remaining pockets of the Catharism that still flourished in the southern village of Montaillou. Thanks to the Bishop's meticulous record-keeping, we have an extraordinary chronicle of the trial of Béatrice. In June 1320, the Bishop took sworn testimony from a local rector of the church of Dalou, who reported a story a member of the congregation had told about Béatrice.[19] Was it a joke? Fournier wanted to know. From her expression and her words, the rector answered, it seemed that she meant it. Brought to testify before Fournier that August and questioned about the story, Béatrice explained:

> When I was a little girl and I was at Celles, about six years before marrying my first husband, the people were hurrying one day to see the body of Christ at the church of this place. I heard a mason (I don't know his name but I think he was Oudin) ask where these people were going. They answered that they were going to see the body of Christ. He said, "They need not hurry so for that because if the body of Christ was as large as the [nearby mountain] Pech de Boulque, it would long ago have been eaten like a pasta!" And I sometimes repeat these words that I heard this man say, without believing them, and I told them at Dalou.[20]

She claimed that she had only passed on a remark that she had once overheard. But incriminating evidence against her was found in the contents of her bag: "two umbilical cords of infants," "cloth stained by blood which seemed to be menstrual blood," "slightly burned incense grains," "a mirror and a small knife wrapped in a piece of linen," "the seed of a plant wrapped in muslin," and "a dried piece of bread," the last item signalling that she had participated in the Cathar ritual of breaking quotidian bread in commemoration of the Last Supper.[21] Béatrice explained that some years prior, a Jewish woman—since converted, or "baptized"—had told her that the menstrual blood, produced by Béatrice's daughter, could, if ingested, prevent a husband from going astray, and that the umbilical cords, belonging to Béatrice's grandchildren, would, if carried on her person, ensure victory should she ever face a legal suit. "I never had the occasion to verify their efficacy," she observed.

The blasphemous joke had poked a hole in the Communion wafer, insinuating that an idolatrous error was being made in identifying it with the substance of the Savior. But it did so in larger service to a reverence for Christ. The denial of the host was an affirmation of the Lord of Hosts. Béatrice was found guilty, among other charges, of blasphemy, and sentenced to death. The sentence was subsequently commuted to wearing a yellow cross on her outer garments for the rest of her days to signify her repentance and admission of error. While *El Shaddai* would have perhaps had her stoned as vengeance, his medieval viceroys wanted her kept alive to testify to the falsity of her former opinion. For Béatrice's blasphemy was not defilement of the sacred Name as such but defiance of the earthly authorities who had installed themselves as the custodians of his truth. Béatrice's judges did not rend their garments in lamentation at the injurious words. Instead they insisted on having them repeated and repeated until the tear in the communal Body of Christ could be sutured shut and orthodoxy restored.

Since the days of the Golden Calf, the criminalization of spiritual blasphemy also faced a serious threat from religious pluralism. There was more than one way to read the Word, more than one way to reverence the bread. Why, then, must we submit to the way preferred by king or bishop? The war against the Cathars, tragically, was anything but the last religious war in Europe's history, as the Lutheran revolt and the splintering of Christendom unleashed cataclysms of violence to make biblical proportions seem quaint. With the proliferation of Christian subcommunities, the question loomed larger and larger. If there were many gods, many dogmas, which of them should enjoy the backing of earthly power? More fundamentally, on what grounds could such a determination be made? On what authority could anyone say that an exercise of coercive force is right or just?

Communal

Such questions preoccupied medieval political thinkers who had to grapple both with the authority of the papacy vis-à-vis secular rulers and the authority of the papacy vis-à-vis the clergy throughout

Christendom. This theoretical discourse was driven by the political controversies of the time. Beginning in the middle of the eleventh century, the Church hierarchy struggled to free itself from interference by secular officials, from the local to the imperial level, who claimed jurisdiction over religious affairs. The key battle in what is now known as the Papal Revolution concerned temporal rulers' claim to responsibility for the appointment or investiture of clergy like bishops and abbots. This so-called "investiture controversy" began in 1076 with Pope Gregory VII excommunicating a defiant Emperor Henry IV, who shot back that the pope had become a "false monk." It ended with the Concordat of Worms of 1122, which liberated the Church from imperial control.[22]

Meanwhile, medieval thinkers were discovering the Roman legal tradition, the systematic study of civil law as codified by Justinian and his officials. In the middle of the twelfth century, Gratian produced his *Concord of discordant canons*, which became commonly known as the *Decretum*. This magisterial collection of original texts on the sorts and sources of law, with commentary by Gratian, created a vibrant new field of jurisprudence wherein "canonists" debated the proper interpretations or glosses on the material of the *Decretum*. Their principal project was the integration of church law with Roman law and the law of the Germanic kings and feudal custom. The latter tradition had a rough notion of popular sovereignty in which the legitimacy of a king's rule flowed from a kind of covenant of trust between himself and his barons and subjects.[23] The actions of a just king enjoy the approval of the people, demonstrated through practical compliance if not formal agreement. Roman jurists, following Cicero and the Stoics, had distinguished human law from "natural law," *ius naturale*, a body of universal, immutable, and divinely authored norms, discoverable by reason, which have moral priority over human law.

Canon lawyers working after the Papal Revolution, in the context of the new political settlements, theorized a distinction between spiritual and temporal power, relying heavily on an influential canon from the *Decretum*, the *Duo sunt*, which was identified as a letter written by

Pope Gelasius I to the newly elected Byzantine Emperor Anastasius I in 494:

> There are two powers, august Emperor, by which this world is chiefly ruled, namely, the sacred authority of the priests and the royal power. Of these, that of the priests is the more weighty, since they have to render an account for even the kings of men in the divine judgment. . . . If the ministers of religion, recognizing the supremacy granted you from heaven in matters affecting the public order, obey your laws, lest otherwise they might obstruct the course of secular affairs by irrelevant considerations, with what readiness should you not yield them obedience to whom is assigned the dispensing of the sacred mysteries of religion.[24]

While Gelasius' letter was an early assertion of papal authority, it also acknowledged a distinct and legitimate sphere of secular authority. As one eighth-century scholar put it: "The secular and the spiritual power are separated; the former bears the sword of death in its hand, the latter bears the key of life in its tongue."[25] In the system of the canonists, the Church would function as a distinct and legally autonomous collective entity with the right to own property, to assemble, to enact and judge its own statutes, and to engage in representative governance, both internal to itself and externally in the broader civil and political order—in a word, it would be a *universitas*, or corporation. In this way, the Papal Revolution and the "twelfth-century renaissance" in law made possible a new vision of society as an aggregate of multiple collective agents, each with its own legal jurisdiction.[26]

Medieval political thinkers were also absorbing newly discovered Arabic and Greek texts of Aristotle's ethics and politics. These, as interpreted by Aquinas and others, informed their model of the proper functions of secular power. The ideal polity did not just provide for security and commerce; it acted to promote the good or virtue of citizens, "the common good." The civil ruler was authorized by the divine and natural law to wield the sword of temporal power for peace, security, and the common good so that the community could live in pursuit of Christian virtue, while the miter of the clergy lent moral strength to his elbow by making it a matter of religious duty to submit "to every ordinance of man for the Lord's sake," as the New Testament instructs.[27]

In the intellectual atmosphere of the thirteenth century, blasphemous affronts to God's authority could be "theorized as an attack upon all secular authority that also derived legitimacy from a supreme creator."[28] The solemn swearing of oaths invoking God's name was important for civil and commercial purposes.[29] To take the Name in vain was to circulate a counterfeit currency that debased the oath. According to one mid-thirteenth-century text, "some oaths are spoken in careless haste, and others deliberately. Men plead that the first is a jesting word; yet it would seem to be a crime. For a plain word, spoken by itself would suffice to convey the jest; therefore the addition of an oath maketh it something more than a jest." An oath is committed to "truth, judgment and justice," yet the "nasty oath hath not such concomitants; wherefore it is perjury."[30]

According to this strand of medieval thought, the blasphemer's offence was less against the godhead—as Aquinas noted, it could hardly be scratched by a sarcastic word—than against the commonwealth. The blasphemer was a threat to the civil peace and security of the community; the sacrilegious was seditious. Disrespect of the authority of the divine undermines public fidelity and respect for the authority of the law. The argument was given its most full-throated expression with the decision in the 1675 case of *R. v. Taylor*.[31] The apparently disturbed John Taylor was indicted for blasphemy for saying that Jesus Christ was a bastard, a "whoremaster," and religion was a "cheat."[32] In a bold juridical stroke that would influence over a century of English common law, the Lord Chief Justice, Sir Matthew Hale, argued:

Such kind of wicked blasphemous words were not only an offence to God and religion, but a crime against the laws, State and government, and therefore punishable in this Court. . . . For to say, religion is a cheat, is to dissolve all those obligations whereby the civil societies are preserved, and that Christianity is parcel of the laws of England, and therefore to reproach the Christian religion is to speak in subversion of the law.[33]

Though Taylor received a relatively light sentence, and within a generation the Aikenhead execution effectively terminated the option of
capital punishment, the English common law offence of blasphemous
libel survived until 2008.

Intuitive as it may seem, Lord Hale's metaphor of faith as "parcel"
of the laws of the land is potentially incoherent. There are at least
three ways to understand it. Christianity somehow might be *identical
to* the law, in which case any challenge to the law would equally be
an affront to Christianity and therefore potentially blasphemous. Or
Christianity somehow might be a *part of* the law, in which case mere
symbolic rejection of Christianity should not be enough to warrant
punishment since mere symbolic rejection of a law is not tantamount
to its violation. The most plausible reading of this argument from subversion, then, is that proper religious belief is an indispensable motive
of citizens' recognition of and respect for the authority of law.

As with the notion of spiritual blasphemy, religious pluralism
presents a challenge to communal blasphemy. Within the Body of
Christ, after reform and counter-reform, doctrines that were once
suppressed and silenced as heretical or blasphemous had come to be
adopted by whole communities and states. In Europe after the 1648
Treaty of Westphalia, different nations acknowledged differing con-
fessions whose beliefs could be blasphemies to each other, and yet
they nevertheless remained stable and even consolidated their power
and extended their regulatory reach. And if respect for the law could
be sustained in a society without the benefit of any Christian dogma
whatever, then the key premise of the argument would be removed.
Cross-cultural counterexamples were impossible to ignore. The
Jews in the midst of the Christian commonwealth were quite conspicuously not a lawless people. Exploration, military conquest, and
commerce brought increasing interpenetration with Hindu, Buddhist,
Confucian, and Islamic cultures.[34] The consolidation of colonial power
in the Middle East and Asia made possible lucrative new markets for
slaves, weapons, steel, textiles, and other goods from Europe.[35] In the
early 1600s, the Dutch signed commercial treaties with Morocco and
Turkey. A number of early writers on toleration were impressed by

the example of civil order under Islam. Roger Williams, the founder of Rhode Island, asked in his *Bloudy Tenent of Persecution for the Cause of Conscience*, published in London in 1644, "whether or no such as may hold forth other worships or religions, Jews, Turks, or anti-christians, may not be peaceable and quiet subjects, loving and helpful neighbours, fair and just dealers, true and loyal to the civil government?"[36] "It is clear they may," he answered, "from all reason and experience in many flourishing cities and kingdoms of the world, and so offend not against the civil state and peace, nor incur the punishment of the civil sword . . ."

Personal

The model of the Law of Moses is, for all its apparent purity, a theory; or at least it entails a theory, and a complex one at that. The theory provides an answer to the question, when is one person justified in exercising power over another? This is the problem of political legitimacy. The Mosaic model supposes that one of the persons is God. This would answer the question only if we assumed that the exercise of power over one person by another is justified just because that other person is God.[37] In Exodus 19, Moses brokers an agreement between the Israelites and *Adonai*, who promises, "Now therefore, if ye will obey my voice indeed, and keep my covenant, then ye shall be a peculiar treasure unto me above all people." The people accept the Covenant at Sinai, so the story goes. If the story makes sense to readers, it is because we have some sense of what makes a covenant worthy of assent and binding commitment. If the people are to have good reason to consent to the compact, and to remain bound by it, then at the very least their interests must be served by it. Consent must not be irrational or imprudent. And so, we assume that *Adonai* keeps his word, or at least is not a notorious covenant-breaker. God's fidelity to his word is part of what is supposed to make him a just patriarch rather than just a tyrant. It may be that given his perfect nature, he always abides by his covenants. Still, the thought that a person is a constant covenant-abider is not the same thing as the thought that the person does what God wills, even if that person is God.

If this is correct, then the problem of political legitimacy cannot be solved simply by supposing that power is exercised by God, or in perfect accord with God's will. We would still need to explain why God wills what he does. Can we understand the foundational story of Moses in another way? Why would the Almighty wish to enter into a compact at all? Had he no concern for the Israelites' welfare, an arrangement for their benefit would have been unappealing—he could have left them to fend for themselves. Had he had no respect for them as a free people, an *agreement* would have been unnecessary—he could have simply compelled compliance with the threat of force. If the Mosaic dispensation was a covenant at all and not an extortion or a subjugation, this can only be because it was a mutually binding commitment entered into by a free people. So, in the biblical text we can read something of the modern insight that legitimacy lies in respecting the equal dignity of persons.

The great seventeenth-century Dutch jurist, Hugo Grotius, reasoned that the Law of Moses, being based in an actual agreement between particular historical persons, did not bind the strangers in their midst, let alone modern strangers such as us:

> But among the Hebrews themselves there always lived some Strangers.
> . . . These, as the Hebrew Rabbins say, were obliged to keep the Precepts
> given to Adam and Noah, to abstain from Idols and Blood, and from
> other Things, which shall be mentioned hereafter in their proper Place;
> but not the Laws peculiar to the Israelites. And therefore, tho' it was not
> lawful for the Israelites to eat of any Beast that died of itself, yet it was
> allowed to the Strangers that dwelt among them. . . . Nor do we find that
> Elisha ever signified to Naaman the Syrian, nor Jonah to the Ninevites,
> nor Daniel to Nebuchadnezzar, nor the other Prophets to the Tyrians, the
> Moabites, and Egyptians, to whom they wrote, that it was Necessary for
> them to receive the Law of Moses.[38]

Yet there is another law, said Grotius, marshalling the resources of medieval legal discourse, a "natural law" which bound Hebrew and stranger, slave and Greek alike. This law is natural because its moral authority flows from special properties that all persons possess independently of positive or human-made law, and therefore it comes prior to positive law in the order of moral justification.

> For though man is an animal, he is one of a special kind, further removed from the rest than each of the other species is from one another. . . . Among the things which are unique to man is the desire for society, that is for community with those who belong to his species—though not a community of any kind, but one at peace, and with rational order.[39]

When other animals sometimes act for the good of their offspring or another member of their species, their behavior proceeds from "some extrinsic principle of intelligence." Human acts of social cooperation "stem from some internal principle, which is associated with qualities belonging not to all animals but to human nature alone." This "care for society in accordance with the human intellect" is the source of natural law.

> Since men not only have this social instinct more than other animals, but also possess the capacity to assess pleasures and pains, both immediately and in the future, and to make judgments about what will conduce to them; we should understand that it is appropriate to human nature rationally to follow good judgment in these matters, and not be disturbed by fear or the lure of immediate pleasure, and that whatever is plainly contrary to good judgment is also contrary to the law of nature.[40]

Through imaginative intelligence we can project ourselves into our possible futures, and so to plan; we can recall ourselves in our actual pasts, and so to regret. Reasoning from general principles, seeking our good within a peaceable community of others, we come to recognize the entitlements that we must mutually accord to each other. We discover our rights.[41]

If we are to live in community, there are some things that we may not do to each other, no matter who might command it: "the Law of Nature is so unalterable," wrote Grotius in 1625, "that God himself cannot change it. . . . So when God commands any Man to be put to Death, or his Goods to be taken away, Murder and Theft do not thereby become lawful, which very Words always include a Crime . . ."[42] This doctrine of natural rights was secular but not irreligious. Even the New Testament acknowledged the existence of moral foundations for law available to those outside the covenant: "For when the Gentiles, which have not the law, do by nature the things contained in the law, these, having not the law, are a law unto themselves: Which shew the work of the law written in their hearts, their conscience also bearing witness, and their thoughts the mean while accusing or else excusing one another."[43]

The theist could maintain that the ultimate author of the law is God. But the Christian natural law tradition already contained the distinct and more precise notion that God is the author of an *agency* with the normative authority to make the law—"natural *ius* is called reason, namely a force of the soul," as the canonist Huguccio stressed.[44] The Creator is less like a national parliament and more like the author of the national constitution that empowers the parliament to legislate. This agency is the faculty of conscience, a faculty of practical reasoning, or thinking about what one has most reason to do. Later Enlightenment thinkers would speak of the capacity for autonomy—self-legislation or self-rule, the distinctively human feat of formulating and acting on the basis of reasons, of knowing and acting in accordance with general principles. Beginning in the early modern period, theorists of secular natural rights could maintain that even while the explanation for the existence of the faculty of conscience may be divine, its normative authority could be free-standing, self-evident, or self-vindicating. Thus, justice might depend on God in the order of explanation without depending on God in the order of justification.[45]

Under the new dispensation of early modern liberal political thought, articulated by Grotius, by Samuel Pufendorf, by Thomas Hobbes and John Locke, law and government were devices designed to protect and secure the morally prior rights of individuals, what would belatedly come to be known as "human rights." These rights were "human rights" because they were equal, inalienable, universal, and paramount. They were paramount in that they took normative precedence over all human-made, positive law; universal, or belonging to all because all partake of the natural capacities of reason and sociality; inalienable, or incapable of being taken away or given away, any more than one's human personhood could be taken or given away; and equal, enjoyed in the same measure by all. The liberal ideal was the realization of a 1,000-year-old text from Isidore of Seville, preserved in the *Decretum*: *omnium una libertas*—the equal liberty of all persons.

According to the liberal ideal, an exercise of a power is legitimate to the extent that free, rational persons would consent to it, forswearing some liberties in order to enter into the fuller freedom of life in a well-ordered community. Power wielded with justness is power that can be justified to each person it touches. Here was the sweeping alternative to the idea that authority flows from the will of God. Moral community is forged of free persons who mutually grant equal standing to one another and political authority is justified not by a covenant with the creator but by a covenant among the created, a covenant in which the lawgiver and the law-receiver are one; into which all persons of conscience may enter; a covenant of strangers.

The shift in Western thought—away from a conception of the law as a source of tribal or community identity to a conception of the law as a rational contrivance for the protection of individual rights—was accompanied by a shift in blasphemy's victim. No longer was the purported injury done to the sacred itself, or to "the common good," but to some identifiable individual or group of individuals. The range of seventeenth-century legislation was "part of a European imposition of varieties of discipline upon unruly populations as an essential by-product of centralizing the state."[46] The English common law offence of blasphemous libel was created in 1617 with the decision that secular authorities could suppress blasphemy because it constitutes a provocation and disturbance of the peace.[47] In the mid-nineteenth century, the jury in the case of *R. v. Hetherington* were told that religious expression is not blasphemous if it is couched in a "sober and temperate and decent style," but only "if the tone and spirit is that of offence, and insult, and ridicule, which leaves the judgment really not free to act, and therefore, cannot be truly called an appeal to the judgment, but an appeal to the wild and improper feelings of the human mind."[48] In his 1883 opinion on the sacrilegious magazine *The Freethinker*, Lord Chief Justice Coleridge held that "if the decencies of controversy are observed, even the fundamentals of religion may be attacked without a person being guilty of blasphemous libel."[49] But if an expression were "calculated and intended to insult the feelings and the deepest religious convictions of the great majority of the persons amongst whom we live," it could be considered blasphemous.[50] Here was a shift from the content of the blasphemy to the character of its expression and the intentions of the speaker.

   This distinction, between the "matter" discussed and the "manner" in which it was discussed, was to have a profound impact on English common law and thereby on colonial governments around the world.[51] The lineage of Pakistan's blasphemy laws, to take one example, can be traced to the "offenses relating to religion" introduced into the Indian Penal Code during British rule, which criminalized acts and words with the "deliberate and malicious intention of outraging the religious feelings" of others.[52] The colonial authorities were particularly concerned to manage and control communal tension and violence. During the military dictatorship's "reforms" of the 1980s, this nineteenth-century European language of personal blasphemy would be spliced together with Islamist content.

   Here, then, was blasphemy against the person. Even as it came to dominate the legal treatment of sacrilegious expression in the West, it bequeathed a complex and divided legacy. It assumed that the problem with blasphemy lies in a failure to show a certain kind of respect to persons. But what kind of respect were people owed? Socially, there was an attitude of favorable regard or esteem for persons of merit, at home in social codes of honor and chivalry belonging to the old aristocratic and patriarchal cultures. Such respect for honor was "vertical"—it was reserved for those possessing some distinction of rank or superiority.[53] Thus, it depended on hierarchies of authority that the egalitarianism of individual rights undertook to undo. The new covenant of the rational contract was a covenant among equals; its impulse was to level honor until all honor became horizontal—honor among (male) equals. The covenant was also accompanied by a new model of a respectable male citizen. The covenant promised safety, security, and peace above courage, sacrifice, and nobility. The master virtue of Hobbesian man was prudence, not honor.[54] Ascending "bourgeois virtues" and Enlightenment egalitarianism collided with older aristocratic codes without washing them away completely.[55] Left behind was a conceptual and legal flotsam. The word for "honor" in the major European languages can denote both the horizontal and vertical senses, the esteem for superior social standing and the acknowledgment of equal moral standing.[56] The same ambiguity survives in the international discourse on "respect" for religious beliefs and "insult" to religious sensibilities.

Another source of ambivalence about respect was philosophical. The doctrine of natural rights was a revolution in thinking about the legitimacy of power in society. It was at the same time a transformation in thinking about the nature of normative authority and the nature of the respect which that authority should command. For what emerged in the work of the twelfth century canonists was a new model of normative authority, which presented the possibility of making the source of reasons internal to the subject's agency: "For some of the Stoics and for Cicero there was a force in man through which he could discern *ius naturale*, the objective natural law that pervaded the whole universe; but for the canonists *ius naturale* itself could be defined as a subjective force or faculty or power or ability inherent in human persons."[57]

This way of thinking about natural law is far from inevitable. It could be that the world presents us not just with a phenomenal order but a normative order. In such a world, states of objective reality—states independent of our agency—by themselves could give us reasons. As theoretical reasoning is a matter of recognizing the empirical facts, practical reasoning would be a matter of recognizing the normative facts and acting accordingly. By moving the locus of natural law from an independent moral order to an agency or "force of the soul," the canonists were pointing away from this kind of external realism about reasons, pointing "inward" toward the subject.[58] In this way of thinking, there are facts about what reasons we have, but these facts are in some sense dependent on the activity of the agent.

The inward turn could be carried in the direction of constructivism about reasons—we have a reason do something when the proper functioning of our practical reason tells us to pursue it. There are no independent normative facts, but we make them so by our practical thinking, constrained by principles of right reason. Practical reason in itself has normative authority. The inward turn could also lead to subjectivism about reasons—we have a reason to do something when we have a certain kind of desire for it. Desires provide the normative force. Reason only tells us what means to pursue in obeying it.[59]

Either way, we confront a quandary. If the moral law is "within" the agent, how do we show proper regard for it? If there are facts about the good or the right that are binding on us independently of what we think about them, then the appropriate response would be to appreciate these facts for their reason-giving force. If, however, facts about the good or the right depend on the activity of the agent, then the appropriate response would be to appreciate that activity of the agent which confers reason-giving force on the good or right. Respect-as-appraisal could be directed at the force of reasons, and respect-as-recognition could be directed at the agency of the reason-giver. Now, suppose we encounter someone whose dearest convictions we appraise as evil, risible, or base. To what extent can we divorce recognition respect from evaluative respect? Can we recognize his equal standing while finding his worldview contemptible? Can we recognize his equal standing while *telling him* we find his worldview contemptible, or does respect demand that in some way we acknowledge the force of what the other finds sacred?

Blasphemy was a crime in search of a victim. With the embrace of pluralism, the secular state, and equal individual rights, Western political culture rejected blasphemy against the divine and blasphemy against the community as targets for criminal law. Beginning with the nameless stranger of Leviticus, annihilated for failing to acknowledge in the Name the source of all moral authority, it came to locate the source of moral authority in the person, neighbor and stranger alike. In the person, the object of reverence, recognition, and appraisal is joined. As the discourse of blasphemy enters international law, it is grappling not with the deference that people owe to their God, but with the deference they owe to each other.

3 Respect

Look at what I suffer, at whose hands, for having respect for piety.

—Antigone

They were warned about the cows. As Odysseus recounts his tale to the Phaeacians in Homer's *The Odyssey*, the nymph Circe foresaw that he and his crew would reach the island of Thrinacia, where "herds of the Sungod's cattle graze, and fat sheep and seven herds of oxen, as many sheep flocks, rich and woolly, fifty head in each. No breeding swells their number, nor do they ever die." If they would leave the beasts untouched, she instructed, "you all may reach Ithaca. . . . but harm them in any way, and I can see it now: your ship destroyed, and your men destroyed as well!"[1] Odysseus shared with his shipmates the warning from Circe, and from the prophet Tiresias: "Friends, we've food and drink aplenty aboard the ship—keep your hands off all these herds or we will pay the price!" For they "belong to an awesome master, Helios, god of the sun who sees all, hears all things."[2] Though the men swore an oath never to harm the herds, after the onboard stores were exhausted, the increasingly mutinous second-in-command, Eurylochus, set his sights on the sacred flocks.

> Listen to me, my comrades, brothers in hardship.
>
> All ways of dying are hateful to us poor mortals,
>
> true, but to die of hunger, to starve to death—
>
> that's the worse of all. So up with you now,
>
> let's drive off the pick of Helios' sleek herds,
>
> slaughter them to the gods who rule the skies up there.
>
> If we ever make it home to Ithaca, native ground,
>
> erect at once a glorious temple to the Sungod,
>
> line the walls with hoards of dazzling gifts!

but if the Sun, inflamed for his longhorn cattle,

means to wreck our ship and the other gods pitch in—

I'd rather die at sea, with one deep gulp of death,

than die by inches on this desolate Island here![3]

The men separated out the finest cattle, surrounded these "splendid beasts with their broad brows and curving horns," offered prayers to the gods, and then slaughtered them. Since "they had no wine to anoint the glowing victims, they made libations with water," broiled the innards, burned the bones, tasted the organs and "hacked the rest into pieces, piercing them with spits." For seven days they feasted on the cattle of the sun, even as Helios cried out to Zeus for vengeance and the hides themselves began to crawl and the hunks of flesh "bellowed out on the spits."[4]

Should Eurylochus have spared the sacred cattle of the sun? Surely he had a prudential reason to refrain, to avoid the disastrous consequences, the fate darkly prophesied for him and his shipmates. He also had reasons of respect. To defy the ban would have been to disrespect Odysseus, and perhaps to dishonor himself and his men. Apart from being an affront to the sacred, an act of sacrilege can be an affront to a person *regarding* the sacred. The modern discourse of sacrilege is personal. It mobilizes the moral notions of respect, insult, offence, and dishonor. It tells us that the wrongness of skewering the cow is the pain caused to the cow's adherents, and that the perpetrator is answerable not to the cow but to them.

The meaning of respect is equivocal. It can summon up the practice of esteeming the other's status in an honor-conscious culture, the practice of appraising the merits of the other's projects, or the practice of recognizing the other's equal standing in the moral community. All of the meanings swirl around the international human rights discourse surrounding blasphemy, religious defamation, and advocacy of religious hatred. Yet human rights must be grounded in the respect of recognition, for human rights must apply to all persons, regardless of their merit or prestige. Honor is bestowed by society; it can be taken away by society. Esteem can be earned; it is not owed to all. What is owed to all, and what cannot be taken away, is the equal standing of persons.

In a multicultural setting, the appeal to a particular honor code will be inadequate to ground a moral accusation of insult via sacrilege. Instead, such an accusation will presuppose shared membership in a moral community forged of equal respect. The argument from disrespect claims that roasting another's cow is an affront, a failure to show due concern and respect for the other. However, it fails to show that concern and respect always require us to refrain from violating the religious sensibilities of others. Rather, offence to others sometimes can be an affirmation of equal respect for them. An argument from incivility holds that constructive public conversation in a democracy—especially one that embraces ethnic and religious subcommunities that are alienated from one another—can only proceed when certain norms of civility are observed. Civility can be said to bar gratuitous insult. But to the extent that norms of civility are enriched with a robust account of reasonableness or special deference to religious conviction, then they beg the questions that are at issue between the blasphemer and believer. On the other hand, there is civic virtue in cultivating an attitude of reasoned skepticism toward public claims—including claims about the sacred—and holding people answerable for them in the space of reasons.

Dishonor

Starvation was far from the first hardship into which Odysseus had led Eurylochus and his men. Odysseus insists on pressing into the cave of the Cyclops, Polyphemus, over their protests, apparently blinded to the danger by his curiosity. The men are trapped in the cave, and in the ensuing ordeal, six are eaten by the Cyclops, and Odysseus reveals his true name and birth, enabling a punishing curse enforced by the beast's father, the god Poseidon. After a subsequent misadventure, when Odysseus manages to spring himself and his remaining crew members from the spells of the enchantress Circe, who had transformed them into pigs, he returns to tell Eurylochus, who had earlier narrowly escaped their fates, and rallies him to rejoin his freed comrades. Eurylochus refuses, calling his captain "hotheaded" and "rash."[5] Odysseus, in response to the accusation, flies into a rage and has to be held back from killing him.

Odysseus took offence, but did Eurylochus wrong him? Did he have reason to feel offended? Grounds for offence are more than feelings of offence. In fact, an insult need not be accompanied by the experience of a negative feeling at all, as when one is the target of an invective in a language that one does not understand. Insult often involves a kind of shock that comes from the sudden disappointment of expectations.[6] Odysseus was accustomed to a certain kind of treatment, a deference to his wishes, and the unexpected deviation by Eurylochus came as a shock. There has been an insult and a cause for complaint on moral grounds only when this deviation somehow constituted a failure to demonstrate to Odysseus the regard or respect he was due.

The Homeric Greeks could frame due respect in the language of *honor*. But not every culture is as honor-conscious. An honor system is culture-relative; it exists within a particular social group, not among human persons as such. The esteem that constitutes honor is not owed to all persons in virtue of their common humanity but granted to some by a community, or "honor group," in accordance with its cultural norms.[7] And as it is granted by the group, it can be rescinded by the group. The distribution of honor tends to be non-egalitarian. Some members of a group will enjoy more honor than others, whether by inherited status or by perceived merit. Honor also tends to be inviolable, eliciting metaphors of purity and defilement, such that one blot on honor can discolor the whole. Infractions on honor are not just transactions between two agents. Reasons of honor are agent-neutral. Whereas a blow to my self-esteem from the neighbor on my left may not alter my standing with the neighbor on my right, a blow to my honor can diminish me in the eyes of the entire community. When I lose "face," it shows to everyone. The respect of honor contrasts most vividly with the respect of recognition, the acknowledgment of the equal moral standing and mutual accountability of another as an autonomous agent. Though my face may be lost, my standing remains because I remain a person, and as a person I am owed respect.

I could mount an argument against honor-consciousness, against placing more weight on the respect of honor than on the respect of appraisal and recognition. The most serious charge against honor would be its gendered and patriarchal nature. Honor is a virtue of *men*. Women's honor, to the extent that it is valued at all, is "defined in terms of women's assigned sexual and familial roles as dictated by traditional family ideology. Thus, adultery, premarital relationships . . . rape and falling in love with an 'inappropriate' person may constitute violations of family honor."[8] Generalizing, I could say that the structure of an honor-conscious culture is immoral because in the place of the moral worth owed to all in virtue of their common humanity, it tends to put social esteem enjoyed—and controlled—by some in virtue of their fortune or distinction. But in saying this I would simply be presupposing an ethics of recognition respect rather than arguing against an ethics of honor respect.[9]

Instead, I will leave this to those within honor-conscious cultures themselves. As honor groups find themselves in cosmopolitan cities, multicultural societies, and global public spheres, they become linked in social cooperation and political deliberation with post-honor groups. When they make accusations against post-honor groups—or divergent honor groups—they commit themselves to the ethics of recognition respect. This happens in cross-cultural accusations of sacrilege. By alleging that a sacrilege impugns their honor, they are presupposing that their interlocutors share equal membership in some form of normative community with them—receiving the spittle of an infant on the face is no dishonor because infants are not full members of the normative community. Yet, when the interlocutor does not occupy the honor community with them, the community of shared membership could only be the moral community, and that community is constructed of the respect of recognition, not the respect of honor. It is the covenant of strangers that extends equal respect to all, even the "dishonored." So, a charge of blasphemy, paradoxically, can be an implicit expression of basic solidarity with the blasphemer, an acknowledgment by the affronted that their antagonist shares with them a community of equal respect.

Disrespect

The most imposing sacred cow in India, some would say, is no cow at all. For perhaps as long as three millennia, life on the subcontinent has been divided by the caste system, with the most grave injustices inflicted on millions of so-called untouchables or *dalits*. India's most famous campaigner for *dalit* rights, B. R. Ambedkar, believed that caste persisted because of a misapprehension of the sacred. In his 1936 book, *The Annihilation of Caste*, he wrote:

> Caste has not the same social significance for non-Hindus as it has for Hindus. . . . Among non-Hindus, caste is only a practice, not a sacred institution. . . . Religion compels the Hindus to treat isolation and segregation of castes as a virtue. . . . Hindus observe caste not because they are inhuman or wrong-headed, but because they are deeply religious. People are not wrong in observing caste. In my view, what is wrong is their religion. Then the enemy is not the people who observe caste, but the Vedas that teach them the religion of caste. . . . Reformers working for the removal of untouchability including Gandhi do not understand that people will not change their conduct until they cease to believe in the sanctity of the Vedas on which their conduct is founded.[10]

In order to annihilate caste, one must "destroy the sacredness and divinity with which caste has become invested. In the last analysis, this means you must destroy the authority of the Shastras and the Vedas."[11] In his agitation for the reform of Hinduism, Ambedkar quite literally destroyed sacred scripture. On 25 December 1927, after leading a procession of dalits to draw water from Chavadar Lake, a source reserved for caste Hindus, Ambedkar scandalized his religious opponents by presiding over the ceremonial burning of a copy of the sacred scripture *Manusmrti*, the ancient "laws of Manu" that give divine sanction to the institution of caste and the supremacy of the Brahmans.[12]

By torching the laws of Manu, did Ambedkar disrespect orthodox Hindus? There are two possible layers of disrespect or insult. First would be an affront to an object of Hindu veneration, which certain

Hindus take as a denigration of their standing in the moral community. If an affront to the dignity of a religious symbol were at the same time an affront to the dignity of those who venerate it, a communicative act of subordination, there would be a *primary insult*. Second, there is the possibility of a kind of meta-insult, an apparent lack of consideration paid to the shock and upset that the primary affront can be predicted to cause the believers—whether or not their assessment of the slight to their dignity is accurate. The blasphemer who goes ahead knowing that this will cause shock and upset would thereby communicate to the believer: your perspective and your concerns do not matter to me. This would be a *secondary insult*. Someone might be innocent of committing a primary insult, but guilty of committing a secondary insult as where he knows his action will be taken as a primary insult and yet he proceeds without due consideration for this fact.

To establish that a primary insult or secondary insult has taken place, it is not enough to show that shock and offence were caused. We can still ask whether, despite the experiences of the offended, the act constituted a failure to show proper respect and concern for anyone. Intention and ignorance matter. Suppose I sit down to sup with an observant Jain and offer him a serving of beef, causing great offence. I may have intended and committed no primary insult, as I have not denied or denigrated the equal moral standing of my companion or all Jains. Whether I am guilty of a secondary insult will depend on whether I should have known of the religious sensibilities of my table-mate. If I am excusably ignorant—having just met the person and having no good reason to be aware of his beliefs—then I cannot be blamed for the offence. (Should I also know that Jains will look more kindly on beans than on potatoes?) If I am culpably ignorant—having thoughtlessly forgotten his earlier explanation of his beliefs to me—then I would be guilty of a secondary insult. Similarly, someone learning a language might repeat a racial or ethic slur without knowing that it constitutes a denigration of standing of the group. If the person can be blamed for not knowing this meaning, then she could be said to be guilty of a primary insult even though she did not intend one.

...sults of the primary variety surely have greater moral gravity than insults of the secondary variety since the secondary depend on the primary for their normative force—if I deny completely your standing in the moral community, then your feeling of offence will be of no concern to me. And yet, primary insults surely admit of a gradation of seriousness. Spitting in someone's face or throwing a shoe at a person would, in certain contexts, constitute primary insults, attacks on his standing. However, these must be less serious insults to a person's standing than publishing an influential treatise on how he is less than human. At the limit, primary insult becomes *hate speech*, the expressive denial or denigration of the basic moral standing of a person or class of persons. Morally acceptable sacrilege crosses the line into hate speech only when it intentionally—or with culpable ignorance—attacks the basic equal standing of persons.

Perhaps the recognition of equal standing is not enough. Perhaps a moral community must be founded on a more robust attitude of respect, respect not only of what is common to all members, but what is distinctive and different in them. On this view, respecting others means more than just acknowledging their shared nature as reason-authoring beings. It means valuing them for the particular identities that they have, showing them a kind of *appraisal* respect.[13] The principle of equal respect seems to suppose that in respecting persons we are affirming the rational agency in them that confers normative force on their reasons. Perhaps instead we need to affirm those reasons themselves. Here is one way that might look. Many of our reasons flow from commitments—including those regarding religion and the sacred—that are not just optional beliefs adopted or rejected by an autonomous self which somehow exists independently of all commitments. Rather, these commitments partially constitute our identities; they make us who we are.[14] Suppose that without a commitment to the Mahar community of his birth—considered to be among the untouchable castes—Ambedkar would be morally fractured, unable to function as an agent and unable to see himself as inhabiting a coherent life. Abandoning the commitment in favor of some competing commitment would be psychologically crippling. Should not the nature of this constitutive commitment determine the kind of respect that he is entitled to receive from others? If we register Ambedkar's worth only *as an autonomous being* and not *as a* Mahar, we are not really registering Ambedkar's worth at all.

Let's grant that the autonomous agent *qua* autonomous agent is a fiction. Every living agent has some particular identities, some commitments without which he would not be capable of giving, receiving, and acting for the sake of reasons. Every autonomous agent is an autonomous *someone*—a Buddhist, a Marxist, a son, a daughter. Still, there are two distinct questions we can ask about this agent, and they must not be conflated. One is the question of identity, the question of what makes him the particular person he is. The other question is the question of his normative standing, the question of what makes it the case that he can make moral demands of others. Confusion arises because these two questions are connected. The answer to the identity question—Who is Ambedkar?—is that he is a Mahar. The answer to the standing question—Why does Ambedkar get to make moral demands of others?—is that he can give and receive reasons. But the standing question, as stated, is ambiguous. If his capacity to give and receive reasons in part depends on his particular identity as a Mahar, then it would seem that the answer to the standing question must include the answer to the identity question. Why does Ambedkar have normative standing? Because he has the capacity to give and receive reasons, and that capacity he has in part because he is a Mahar. Respect for Ambedkar would then entail recognition of his particular identity, and the rejection or denigration of that identity would represent a failure of respect for him.

The ambiguity can be eliminated with this observation: Ambedkar's identity as a Mahar in part explains how he came to be the kind of being that has normative standing, but this identity is *not what makes it the case* that he has equal normative standing. By attributing equal standing to him, we are not committed to a substantive judgment that his identity has equal worth relative to other identities.[15] By the same token, Ambedkar could respect an orthodox, upper-caste Hindu neighbor as fellow reason-guided agent and recognize that he owes this agency in part to his particular identity, without thereby being committed to thinking that this identity is as worthy as his own, or any other. After all, the identity without which his neighbor's agency would disintegrate might be the identity of an intolerant bigot.

Analogously, suppose you are fluent in English and Hindi, and you are conversing with someone fluent in English only. By respecting his standing as a conversation partner, you are at the same time acknowledging him as a competent user of English. Without this competence, he would not be a conversation partner for you. Yet, it is not in virtue of sharing English that you have equal standing as conversation partners, but *in virtue of having a common language.* Were your interlocutor a Hindi speaker, he would have no less standing. Further, your acknowledgment of him as an English-speaking conversation partner is not yet an affirmation of the advantages, attractions, or worth of English relative to Hindi or any other language. Indeed, the topic of conversation might well be the advantages of Hindi over English. There is no contradiction in that. You can respect his standing, and acknowledge that he owes his standing to his being an English user, while at the same time criticizing English use relative to Hindi use. In this way, the positive evaluative respect owed to someone's particular identity just in virtue of its contribution to his standing need not attribute to it any worth beyond its contribution to his standing.

However, there may well be grounds for an independent source of appraisal respect. Even the slightest historical consciousness suggests grounds for adopting a presumption that everyone's religious or cultural identity contains *something* worth caring about, the presumption that "all human cultures that have animated whole societies over some considerable stretch of time have something important to say to all human beings."[16] Yet you could adopt this presumption in relation to identities you have yet to encounter while at the same time exercising critical judgment about the substantive worth of the identities before you. To acknowledge that any of the identities you have yet to encounter may have equal worth is not to acknowledge that all of those you have encountered do have equal worth. Together, these attitudes—the presumption that an identity contains something worth caring about, and the acknowledgment that an identity makes a contribution to equal standing—can be called narrow appraisal respect.

It might be objected that existing in moral community with others entails more than just respect. It entails care or concern. We have concern for someone when we intrinsically value her welfare or interests; when we want, for its own sake, that she is benefited, that her life goes well. Surely, we do not give our neighbors the same care we give our friends and loved ones. Nevertheless, unless we are ethical egoists, we are committed to some basic level of equal concern for others. Morality, it is near-universally agreed, has an essential connection to impartiality or universality. To think morally is to adopt what Thomas Nagel has called an "impersonal standpoint." To adopt the impersonal standpoint is to "focus on the raw data provided by the individual desires, interests, projects, attachments, allegiances and plans of life that define the personal points of view of the multitude of distinct individuals, ourselves included."[17] When viewed impersonally, some of these things do not cease to matter. Rather, it appears that "they matter not only *to* particular individuals or groups." If anything matters to you personally, it is hard to avoid the conclusion that some things matters impersonally. What matters to you personally is raising a child, fighting injustice, making a discovery or creating something beautiful. But part of why you think the pursuit is worthy of your commitment is that you think it is worthy of anyone's commitment, which is to say, worthy. Its value from an impersonal standpoint makes sense of its values from a personal standpoint. "But since the impersonal standpoint does not single you out from anyone else, the same must be true of the values arising in other lives. If you matter impersonally, so does everyone."

If this is correct, then a moral relationship with another requires not just respect, but some minimal form of impartial concern for whatever impersonal value your life has in common with the other, be it interests, well-being, happiness, or virtue. Morality does not commit you to thinking that no one is more important than anyone else, impersonally, but only that "at the baseline of value in the lives of individuals, from which all higher-order inequalities of value must derive, everyone counts the same."[18] Although concern may be motivated by an attitude of empathy toward the other, it is agent-neutral in the sense that it is an appreciation of a good that *anyone* from an impersonal standpoint has a reason to appreciate. The welfare of the other is not just a good for you, but a good, impartially.

Respect for a person can stand in tension with care or concern for her. She may want something that we sincerely believe will not be to her benefit. "We may rightly think, for example, that unhealthy habits are harmful for someone and thus contrary to her welfare, but we may think as well that respect tells against exerting undue pressure to induce her to change." In such a case, concern "may lead us to want her to change, and to want to help her do so, even while respect for her dignity restrains us."[19] How far may concern take us in thinking and acting contrary to her autonomous choices? For purposes of understanding the morality of personal blasphemy and sacrilege, it is enough to show that concern can justifiably bring us to the point of rejecting an identity that constitutes her agency.

It is crucially important that recognizing a person's standing does not simply amount to endorsing her existing identities. Just because a commitment is constitutive of identity does not mean it is worth having, all things considered. Losing an identity can be morally disorienting and psychologically crippling. But persisting in one can sometimes be worse. "Even when shedding unsupportable constitutive values is painful and wrenching, even damaging, it may still be a valuable thing to do. It may be wrenching and dislocating to extricate one's self from a bad marriage, but it is not obviously better to remain in it."[20] Accordingly, the decision to defile a sacred value can be justified by concern for the other: the conviction that her interests matter, and that her interests are not being well-served by the particular religious identity she inhabits. This same form of concern is at work when we advise a friend or loved one to forsake a doomed and destructive marriage, even though this advice may be wounding to her and subversive of her identity as spouse. Like all of us, she has multiple practical identities, and so there are others available to her self-understanding as an agent.[21]

In sum, we enter into moral community with others by engaging in a complex relationship in which we adopt attitudes of (1) recognition respect for their status as persons to whom we are mutually answerable; (2) narrow appraisal respect for the particular commitments and identities that have contributed to their agency; and (3) impartial concern for their interests. These attitudes are consistent with causing offence and, in some cases, insult to others. In some circumstances, as when the other is married to a monster or worshipping an idol, they require it.

Accountability

Is it okay to insult the religious because they chose to be that way? Some commentators think that religiously offensive speech is different in kind from racist hate speech because religious belief is the product of choice, whereas race is an inherited and involuntary condition, an "immutable characteristic."[22] This argument is misleading on two counts. First, it is factually flawed. While voluntary choice may be essential to salvation in Protestant Christianity, it is much less important in other traditions. Second, the argument is morally specious. The voluntariness of a person's condition or group membership by itself does nothing whatever to justify a different standard of treatment of that person. Consider a biracial individual who decides to identify publicly with the minority racial group in his lineage. Discrimination against him would not be less odious in virtue of the fact that his identity was chosen by him rather than bestowed on him. The invidiousness of the discrimination rather depends on the fact that it is based on features that are morally irrelevant, such as his skin color.

In order to differentiate morally acceptable sacrilegious speech from hate speech, we do not need to rely on a culturally idiosyncratic notion of religion, or a specious distinction between chosen and inherited conditions. We need only to distinguish between conditions that exist in the space of reasons and those that do not. What is the difference between the mockery of the mentally disabled and the mockery of corrupt politicians? In a way not true of the disabled, the social identity of a corrupt politician is defined by certain *commitments*. From a moral point of view, what distinguishes the conditions that simply befall you—such as your genetic endowment—from the commitments that you live by is the presumption that you are answerable to others for your commitments. They are the kinds of things for which reasons can be requested and given. Here a "reason" is not restricted to matters of logic, calculation, and ratiocination, but includes any consideration that is taken to count in favor of an attitude or action. In this sense, reason does not preclude emotion: a feeling of terror can be a reason to flee and an emotion of loyalty or affection can be a reason to stay. What is essential to reasons is their normative force. They speak to us of how we *ought* to orient ourselves in the world. To live by a commitment is implicitly to undertake the obligation to vindicate that commitment before other persons by appeal to considerations that count in favor of it. These considerations may not in the end be persuasive to others, but they must be such that others are at least able to understand how they could be reasons for us. In a way not true of the biological accidents of our birth, our commitments exist in "the space of reasons."

Religious identities can occupy the space of reasons even when they are inherited and not chosen. This is because they contain certain publicly accessible claims about the history, nature, and destiny of the world, as well as moral attitudes about the best to which human beings can aspire. As commitments that may be unchosen, religious identities are something like nationalities. While my US citizenship was bestowed at birth and not chosen by me, in public life this identity implies certain commitments, like a commitment to individualism or to a market economy. Especially when I am interacting with publics outside of the country, I can expect to be called upon to explain or to vindicate these commitments, or in the case that I disavow them, to explain how and why I disavow them. In neither case will it be a fully satisfactory answer to these calls to say,

"This is just the way I am." My particular identity as citizen remains in the space of reasons.

It might be objected that we can only be responsible for our free choices. In fact, we can be responsible not just for our actions and choices, but for anything that is attributable to us for the purposes of moral appraisal, whatever is the proper object of the "reactive attitudes" of others. Resentment, anger and, on other occasions, guilt, gratitude, forgiveness, solidarity, and love are "natural human reactions to the good or ill will or indifference of others toward us, as displayed in *their* attitudes and actions."[23] They reflect "how much we actually mind, how much it matters to us, whether the actions of other people—and particularly of *some* other people—reflect attitudes toward us of goodwill, affection, or esteem on the one hand or contempt, indifference, or malevolence on the other."[24]

What is it that provides the right kind of link between the attitudes and the agent who is the subject of moral praise, blame, or indifference? What makes them attributable to him for the purposes of moral appraisal? Is it that we care about actions that signal a vice or virtue of the agent's character? If that were so, and the actions were just a sign of a character defect, such as faulty desires, then it is hard to see why the action would provide *additional* grounds for blame. The defect would be blameworthy, whether or not it manifested in action.[25] What else could it be about actions that makes them appropriate objects of moral appraisal? Actions are typically thought to be the product of a pairing of a desire and a belief about how to actualize that desire. Perhaps the link is that one's character is comprised of various desires and beliefs that, while not defects in and of themselves, can in combination give rise to defective actions. The puzzle here is how a collection of states that in themselves are not relevant to moral appraisal would, just by combining, result in something that is relevant to moral appraisal. What this proposal needs is "some account of what it is that ties all of these various desires, beliefs and dispositions together as the desires, beliefs, and dispositions of *an agent*, and why their 'resulting in' some action on a given occasion should be thought to reflect poorly *on him or her*."[26]

The leading candidate is choice. A person's pride reflects on him because it is the product of earlier voluntary choices, or because he has reflected on it and endorsed it, or because it is something that can be modified by his choices.[27] We can hold him responsible for those things about himself that he has chosen. The problem with choice-based accounts is that in morally appraising, we take into consideration "a wide variety of attitudes and mental states, many of which do not arise from conscious choice or decision, and many of which do not seem to fall under our immediate voluntary control."[28] The recklessness of which Eurylochus accused Odysseus, for example, consisted in the fact that he *failed to notice* important features of his situation, he spontaneously responded to the scene with curiosity and eagerness, and it did not occur to him to contemplate the risks to the crew. Neglecting things, failing to have certain thoughts, and sponta- neously reacting are not exemplars of choice. Nevertheless, they are things for which we can be held responsible.

If mental events like these are relevant to praise and blame, it is not because they are under the direct supervision of our conscious will, but because they fall under the purview of reason. They are the kinds of things for which reasons can be given, and therefore the kinds of things for which we are *answerable* to others. What Eurylochus resents about Odysseus' cavalier attitude at Polyphemus' lair is that it implies a commitment to regarding his own interests or good name as more valuable than the lives of his crewmembers. This is not to say that Odysseus consciously entertained the commitment as a reason for this attitude, or the fateful actions that followed from it. Rather, he acted impulsively. Nevertheless, the reason is what makes sense of his behav- ior, on the assumption that he is basically reason-guided or responsive to reasons. This assumption could fail, as when the song of the Sirens takes such control of Odysseus that his decisions are no longer being produced by a process responsive to reason. When he is listening to the Sirens instead of listening to reason, Odysseus is not responsible for his actions and must simply be lashed to the mast. Under normal circumstances, however, by taking Odysseus to be a person, his crew adopts an interpretive stance toward him in which they treat him as basically reason-guided unless they are forced to conclude otherwise by the evidence of his behavior.

Holding others accountable for their commitments is a way of respecting their natures as reason-authoring creatures, their equal standing as persons who are no less capable of making up their minds than ourselves. By asking the venerator of the cow, rather than the cow, to account for its veneration, we are presupposing that the venerator shares with us the space of reasons. Thus, an affront to what is held sacred by others can be, paradoxically, a way of affirming their equal membership in moral community.

The susceptibility to criticism by others is a condition of existing in community with them. The freedom to move through the public spaces of a city, to go to the market or pick up the day's news, brings with it the exposure to a certain degree of scrutiny by others. My freedom to walk the same streets as you do is made possible in part by the fact that, were I to tread on you, I would stand accountable to you for that. My accountability is inseparable from my liberty. In a similar way, my freedom to live by some orientation to the sacred is made possible by a condition—the mutual recognition of equal moral standing—that at the same time makes me accountable to others for the commitments this orientation makes.

None of this exculpates the gratuitously offensive. In the course of ordinary social life, it is assumed that we all have reasons to refrain from insults both primary and secondary. A blasphemy that incurs no primary insult, no denigration to the standing of persons, may yet incur a secondary insult if the blasphemer proceeds without consideration for the hurt that his blasphemy will cause. The blasphemer has a reason not to insult. Still, what we should do is a matter of what we have *most* reason to do. The fact that I have a reason not to insult you does not show that I have most reason not to insult you. The reason not to insult might be defeated by more powerful countervailing reasons. For instance, I may be compelled to avoid starvation. I may think that your claims about the sacred deserved to be raked across the coals of public conversation. Or I may be compelled by my own, competing vision of what genuinely is sacred.

The Symmetry Thesis

In place of the smouldering *Manusmrti*, Ambedkar offered a compet-ing vision that found sanctity in individual human personhood. It is not the authority of the Vedas, but the individuality of the person that is inviolable, and therefore properly sacred. The compulsory social stratification and inequality inherent in the castes is incompatible with the sacredness of the person. The proper response to this central value is to create social conditions of equality and social mobility: "Once the sacredness of human personality is admitted the necessity of liberty, equality and fraternity must also be admitted as the proper climate for the development of human personality."[29] Thus, in an important sense, Ambedkar was arguing that the caste system is an affront to the sacred.

Arguably, Ambedkar did not impugn the basic dignity or stand-ing of Hindus, going out of his way to denigrate their religion instead.[30] He did, however, intentionally rain down secondary insults on Hindus, but far from doing so gratuitously, or self-servingly, or simply because his right to freedom of speech allowed him to do so, Ambedkar dared to offend in the service of what he deemed sacred. The charge is often leveled by believers against desecraters that they irresponsibly exercise their legal freedom of expression in a way that treads on the sensibilities of others. But the example of Ambedkar shows that a perfectly symmetrical charge can be leveled against them. Ambedkar could maintain that orthodox Hindu expressions affirming the caste system constitute affronts to the sanctity of human personhood. He would have no less cause for insult. He would have as much ground to accuse them of an irresponsible misuse of their right of free speech.

This symmetry extends not just as far as the dissident Hindu or Buddhist, but equally to the atheist and secularist. Goparaju Ramachandrarao, or Gora, a botanist who emerged from the Gandhian movement, founded a center devoted to "positive atheism" in the southern state of Andhra Pradesh that still conducts inter-caste and casteless marriages and "cosmopolitan dinners" open to all. Gora's

autobiography recounts the moment at the age of 26 when he repudi-
ated his Brahmin identity:

> The full moon of August was the day each year when the sacred thread was
> ceremoniously changed for a new one. On that day in 1928, my father held
> out a thread to me and asked me to wear it as a matter of religious discipline
> and respect for the rules of caste. I had not discarded the thread wholly so
> far. I was only indifferent to it. But my father's conventional discipline chal-
> lenged my atheistic leanings. Politely I told him, "Father, I have great regard
> for you. But I have no respect for caste. For the past two or three years I
> have been indifferent to wearing the thread, which is a symbol of a caste.
> But on this day, when the thread is changed for a new one, let me make up
> my mind and be honest to my convictions. I'll discard the thread wholly
> from today."[31]

Gora's father, enraged, ordered him to wear the thread. When
Gora held firm, he was ejected from the family home and excom-
municated: "I was outcaste." Gora's renunciation of his hereditary
privilege was at the same time a rejection of the alleged sanctity of
caste. His sacrilege was not just an exercise in free speech but an
expression of his convictions of conscience about what is and what
is not part of a divinely consecrated normative order. It was inseparable from an egalitarian moral outlook that would come to shape
his life projects. With regard to the ethics of insult and respect,
Gora's conviction that caste is not a part of a divinely consecrated
normative order was on a par with his father's conviction that it is.
Whatever deference or consideration his father deserved in virtue
of his claim about the sacred, Gora deserved equally in virtue of his
claim about the sacred.

If the symmetry between the positions of the desecrator and the
believer is not widely appreciated, it is only because certain claims
about the sacred have historically enjoyed the advantage of being
bundled together with systems dubbed "religions." But a sacred good
is not worth caring about simply because it is linked to "religion." It
might be objected that Gora's father's claim about the sacredness of

caste deserved more moral deference than Gora's claim because the elder's claim was more central to his identity. More generally, one might object that the person who makes a positive claim about the sacred deserves more respect than the person who makes a negative claim. Gora's story belies this objection, for his desecration of caste was no less vital to his moral life than was his father's affirmation of it. No one has any more or less license than anyone else to speak on behalf of the sacred or against its misappropriation. The desecrator can be the believer, and the believer the desecrator.

Any desecrater is answerable to others. It is incumbent on her, whenever possible, to avoid primary insult and to anticipate or answer the charge of secondary insult by demonstrating an attitude of concern for the hurt and affront that may be caused to believers. This is the best that can be done to dispel the impression that the desecration was undertaken without due consideration for their interests. The prima facie duty to refrain from gratuitous insult with regard to their sacred goods is no different from the duty to refrain from gratuitous insult with regard to their parents, clan or country in that each is grounded in the commitment to showing them equal concern and respect. However, this duty to avoid gratuitous insult falls no less on traditional believers than on religious minorities and secular persons.

Incivility

The foregoing exploration has supposed that blasphemous expression can have a place in constructive conversation. Yet, it might be objected that constructive conversation can only occur when certain norms of civility are observed, and those norms of civility must rule out the intentional roasting of the sacred cows of others. Consider the conversation that takes place in the direct democratic forum of a community meeting. When a community gathers to discuss matters of local governance, it gathers on the assumption that all are equals and that each will express him or herself honestly and freely on these matters. "The basic principle is that freedom of speech shall be unabridged. And yet the meeting cannot even be opened unless, by common consent, speech is abridged."[32] Paradoxically, freedom of speech—the freedom of each participant to make meaningful contributions to a constructive conversation—is made possible by "rules of order" that constrain speech, as Alexander Meiklejohn observes:

> debaters must confine their remarks to the "questions before the house." If one man "has the floor," no one else may interrupt him except as provided by the rules. . . . If a speaker wanders from the point at issue, if he is abusive or in other ways threatens to defeat the purpose of the meeting, he may be and should be declared "out of order." . . . And if he persists in breaking the rules, he may be "denied the floor" or, in the last resort "thrown out" of the meeting. . . . The town meeting, as it seeks for freedom of public discussion of public problems, would be wholly ineffectual unless speech were thus abridged. . . . It is not a dialectical free-for-all. It is self-government.[33]

In a democratic society, it could be argued, conversation on matters of public concern must be governed by similar speech-abridging rules of civility. By conforming their public expressions to civility rules, citizens make possible constructive dialogue and thereby contribute to the practices of democratic self-governance. In this way, civility is an indispensable civic virtue in a democratic society. "There are no legal limits to free speech, but there are civic limits," Tariq Ramadan has remarked. "In any society, there is a civic understanding that free speech should be used wisely so as not to provoke sensitivities, particularly in hybrid, multicultural societies we see in the world today. It is a matter of civic responsibility and wisdom, not a question of legality or rights."[34] On this view, citizens may have the legal right to be uncivil, but they have a civic, moral duty to be civil, and this duty gives them a powerful reason not to blaspheme.

The problem with the argument from incivility is that the "norms of civility" that are brought to bear on blasphemy are not purely procedural and value-neutral. While the rules of order of a community meeting, such as "don't interrupt one who has the floor," may be relatively non-controversial, any deliberative body deliberating on interesting issues for an interestingly diverse population will have to make some substantive assumptions about what counts as a reasonable contribution, what counts as purely abusive speech, and which parties deserve civil treatment. Is an opening prayer a helpful contribution? Is satire always uncivil? Should uncivil people be treated with civility? These assumptions will vary depending on one's cultural practices, moral orientation and religious worldview.

To see this, consider the sacred bean. The sixth-century Greek mathematician Pythagoras is believed to have urged his followers to abstain from beans. Apparently, the Pythagoreans, along with the Orphics, thought that they were "ensouled" as part of the cosmic drama of reincarnation. One Orphic verse informs us, "Eating beans and eating the heads of one's parents amounts to the same thing," and Aristotle attributes to the Pythagoreans the view that the bean, the only plant "without joints," resembles "the mouth of Hades" through which souls ascend back to life on earth.[35] Pythagoras is said to have conducted experiments revealing that masticated bean matter left out in the sun starts to smell like semen and that a bean blossom buried for 90 days takes the form of a child's head or a woman's vagina.[36] Imagine a band of neo-Pythagoreans bent on reviving a reverence for beans in contemporary times. Seen through the revivalists' vision of the sacred, mainstream society would cry out for radical reform. Cans of soup in supermarkets would be like row upon row of violent pornography in full view of children; Indian cookbooks would read like blueprints for moral degradation. The neo-Pythagoreans would disrupt chili contests in Texas and call for economic sanctions against the *mangiafaglioni* of Tuscany, all by appealing to an outrage against their spiritual sensibilities.

I will leave to others to decide whether the sacred beliefs of the familiar world faiths make more sense than those of the fictional neo-Pythagoreans. The point is rather that the neo-Pythagoreans could claim that you and I are obstructing civil dialogue, and therefore forsaking our civic duty, by refusing to redact our soup recipes and persisting in our omnivorous ways. When they assert that our actions are not merely ignorant or wicked but *uncivil*, they might be claiming that we have violated a procedural rule of conversation by being gratuitously insulting or that our contributions are grossly unreasonable. They might conclude that we are beyond the pale of conversation altogether, undeserving of civil treatment because we are collaborators in a genocide of souls. If you and I have no sympathy for these suggestions, it is probably because we are not convinced that eating a bean is the same thing as eating the heads of one's parents. Even if the reverence for living things and their origins could in some form be appreciated, the neo-Pythagorean cult's bizarre investment of this reverence in the token of the bean would be morally unintelligible to most of us. In short, we would think the neo-Pythagoreans are misguided, and therefore we would disagree with them about whether we are being uncivil toward them, and perhaps even about whether they deserve to be treated with civility. We would not simply accept their norms of civility. Our disagreement would cut across even those norms.

I will not attempt to deduce some universal norms of civility to which every rational being must assent. But if I did, I would be making a contribution to public discourse that could be contested by someone else. That contestation would be a sign that we share a democratic way of life. When agents make assertions about what is and what is not civil or reasonable, these assertions do not stand outside of the public contests over the good and the sacred, adjudicating them like impartial referees. They are moves within the contests. The disputes cannot be settled by asserting that the blasphemer has a civic duty to defer to the attitudes of the believer, for the disputes would then come to include the question of whether civic duty demands such deference.

Surely there are some incontestable procedural rules, presuppositions without which an interaction between persons would not be discourse, "communicative action," or conversation at all.[37] By entering into conversation, persons presuppose at least provisionally that they are talking about a common subject matter; that each is relevantly equal in that each is entitled to speak on the matter; that each is capable of offering and being motivated by reasons; that each aims at motivating the other with reasons rather than coercion or manipulation. When we adopt the "conversational stance" with someone, constraints such as these are not optional.[38] They are constitutive of the stance. Of course, we may not always have most reason to adopt the conversational stance with someone. We may have most reason to confound or confine him, or to run away. The rules of chess are presupposed by those who are playing chess, but they cannot tell us that we must play chess. Yet if we are committed to granting equal moral standing to all persons, extending them equal respect, then we do have a powerful reason to extend the conversational stance as widely as possible, for there is no better way to respect their autonomy, recognize their identities, and give consideration to their interests than to talk to them. However, the conversational stance alone does not determine whether and when we may shock or offend our interlocutors, nor when we have most reason to forsake the conversational stance for some other kind of expressive action. Thus, it leaves open plenty of space for sacrilegious expression, and for dispute about whether sacrilegious expression is inherently uncivil.

This is not to say that there are no constraints on public discourse beyond the procedural norms of the conversational stance. If the arguments of the previous sections are correct, then the blasphemer, like his interlocutor, has a prima facie moral reason not to engage in insults, primary or secondary, as these betray a failure of due respect for the other. So, if the protest of incivility amounts to a charge of insult, it is subject to the points and limitations canvassed above. If, however, the protest of incivility amounts to something more than the injunction against insult, it must be by introducing some additional, morally substantive notions. Labeling these notions "civility" will not dissolve the substantive dispute. The appeal to civic virtue is not enough to prohibit expression that some find blasphemous. On the other hand, it can be argued that democratic civic virtue presents a positive reason to blaspheme in some cases.

The impulse to extend the conversational stance harmonizes with the commitment to a democratic way of public life as the way of life that seeks relentlessly to subject all power to conversation. This commitment to a democratic way of life does generate a civic duty to hold people answerable for the claims they make whenever we believe these claims are of public interest. Matters of public interest include not just public health, safety, and legal rights, but more fundamental ideas about the moral basis for social cooperation, notions of fairness, conceptions of the citizen, ideals of human excellence, models of authority, justification, punishment, and redemption. A claim touching on a matter of public interest invites the question of normative authority: Why should anyone accept that? In a democratic society, we should hope wherever possible to accept claims without a brute appeal to authority or force.

Life in any actual human community is a near-continual negotiation over the proper exercise of power and authority. Ideally, the democratic way of life is a raft of social practices in which matters of public interest are determined to the greatest extent possible by reasoned deliberation and the free interplay of interests rather than by raw authority or domination. Therefore, in a democratic society, an attitude of reasoned skepticism toward public claims is a civic virtue, a complex disposition and habit of citizens that reinforces deliberative practices, and in turn is reinforced by them. It is a civic virtue to subject public claims to interrogation in the space of reasons. When blasphemy serves such conversation, by engaging in the space of reasons with a commitment about the sacred, it constitutes an exercise of a civic virtue crucial to democracy.

Here, then, are three positive reasons in favor of religious criticism, even when it offends: treating believers as equals in the moral community, exercising the civic virtue of holding public claims accountable in the space of reasons, and defending one's own vision of the sacred. In exchange for the freedom of belief afforded us in an open society, we are obligated to accept a certain degree of public scrutiny of our beliefs. The very same principles that allow us to live our lives according to our beliefs give others the right to question them, and sometimes even to desecrate them. It is true, as we often hear, that with freedom of speech comes responsibility, the responsibility to use that freedom judiciously in a way that recognizes the equal moral standing of others. But the freedom of belief also carries with it responsibility, the responsibility to enter the space of reasons and abide by the public accountability that reigns there. The very same freedom that lights up this space for belief also creates belief's shadow, its inseparable companion, blasphemy.

4 Rights

> *The order did not come from God. Justice, that dwells with the gods below, knows no such law.*
>
> —*Antigone*

The Council of Love was never seen. The film was based on *Das Liebeskonzil*, a blasphemous nineteenth-century play by Oskar Panizza. Published in print in Zurich in late 1894, *Das Liebeskonzil* was a mordant anti-Catholic satire. Panizza imagines heaven populated by a decrepit and feeble God, a wilful and lascivious Mary, and a cretinous Jesus who has been depleted by the continual consumption of his flesh and blood by his loving flock. It is 1495, the year Rodrigo Borgia is elected Pope Alexander VI. Scandalized by the orgiastic excesses they observe below in the corrupt Borgia papacy, the dysfunctional Holy Family solicit advice on punishment from the Devil, who conceives of the sexually transmitted disease. His daughter will be dispatched to spread what is unmistakably syphilis to worldly rulers, the papal court, bishops, holy orders, and the masses—that is, after sharing a lustful kiss with the Mother of God in Act Four. In exchange for his idea, Satan requests freedom of thought and speech. Mary says she will think about it. Meanwhile, the author was put on trial for blasphemy.

Ninety years later, a film version of Panizzi's play was to be screened at the Otto-Preminger-Institut in Innsbruck, Austria. The film, directed by Werner Schroeter, captures a performance of the play by the Teatro Belli in Rome and places it within recreated scenes of Panizza's blasphemy trial. At the request of the Innsbruck diocese of the Roman Catholic Church, on 10 May 1985 the public prosecutor charged the institute with "disparaging religious doctrines" under section 188 of the Penal Code. After a private screening by a regional judge, the film was seized. Patrons who arrived for the screening on 13 May instead heard a reading of the script.

When in Paris in December 1948 the Universal Declaration of Human Rights was adopted by representatives of 48 nations, it echoed the language of two revolutionary declarations before it: the Declaration of Independence and the Declaration of the Rights of Man and of the Citizen: "All human beings are born free and equal in dignity and rights." Yet gone from this document were the aspirations of particular nations; gone were "men." "Everyone is entitled to all the rights and freedoms set forth in this Declaration, without distinction of any kind, such as race, color, sex, language, religion, political or other opinion, national or social origin, property, birth or other status." According to the doctrine of the Declaration, all nation states were obligated to respect the human rights of all those within their borders.

The norms of the Universal Declaration were embodied in a series of "covenants," most importantly, the International Covenant on Civil and Political Rights (ICCPR) and the International Covenant on Economic, Social and Cultural Rights, both of which were adopted in 1966 and entered into force in 1976. Together, with the "optional protocols," international treaties by which states voluntarily consent to an enforcement mechanism, the Declaration and the covenants comprise an International Bill of Rights.

These rights are put forward as equal, inalienable, universal, and normatively preeminent, but they are not ahistorical or transcendent. The International Bill of Rights is a document of struggle, a historical record of the demands for equal concern and respect made by individuals against power-wielding entities with society-wide reach: nation states, religions, and profit-seeking corporations.[1] They are a chronicle of the assertions of autonomy by people confronting coercion and control under particular historical circumstances. One article—"No one shall be subjected to torture or to cruel, inhuman or degrading treatment or punishment"—reflects the moral claims against governments by actual victims of torture and their loved ones. Another—"No one shall be imprisoned merely on the ground of inability to fulfil a contractual obligation"—reflects the historical reality of debtor's prisons. Yet another asserts a right to "rest, leisure, and reasonable limitation of working hours and periodic holidays with pay"—a response to the exploitation of the economically vulnerable by private enterprises.

The International Bill of Rights is inscribed with the lives of workers, prisoners, slaves, and victims of torture, and also with the lives of blasphemers, of Thomas Aikenhead, Béatrice de Planissoles, and the Ahmadiyya of Pakistan. During the drafting of Article 18 of the Universal Declaration—which provides freedom of thought, conscience and religion—it was an Ahmadi Muslim, Muhammad Zafrulla Khan, who came to the aid of the proposal by the Lebanese delegate Charles Malik, a Christian, to include the right to change one's religion or belief, a proposal categorically opposed by Saudi Arabia.[2] The right to commit sacrilege, it would seem, should be secured under international law by the force of these provisions. If so, then insofar as nation states are bound to implement the provisions of international law at all, their constitutional and statutory law would be bound to protect this right.

Following a series of appeals, in 1994 the case of Otto-Preminger-Institut v. Austria came before the European Court of Human Rights in Strasbourg. The applicant alleged a breach of its right to freedom of expression under Article 10 of the European Convention for the Protection of Human Rights and Fundamental Freedoms, the regional human rights treaty for members of the Council of Europe which expresses the norms of the International Bill of Rights. Article 10, paragraph 2 permits limitations on the right of freedom of expression only when they are "prescribed by law" and "necessary in a democratic society" for "the prevention of disorder or crime" or "the protection of the reputation or rights of others," among other conditions.

The Court saw itself as "weighing up the conflicting interests" between Article 10 freedoms and "the right of other persons to proper respect for their freedom of thought, conscience and religion." It found no breach, and instead vindicated Austria's blasphemy law. The judges detected in the European Convention a "right to respect for one's religious feelings," claiming that "in extreme cases the effect of particular methods of opposing or denying religious beliefs can be such as to inhibit those who hold such beliefs from exercising their freedom to hold and express them."[3]

The Court cannot disregard the fact that the Roman Catholic religion is the religion of the overwhelming majority of Tyroleans. In seizing the film, the Austrian authorities acted to ensure religious peace in that region and to prevent that some people should feel the object of attacks on their religious beliefs in an unwarranted and offensive manner.[4]

The Court remarked upon a lack of "a uniform conception of the significance of religion in society" across Europe, and reasoned that national authorities "better placed than the international judge" to resolve conflicts of fundamental freedoms "in the light of the situation obtaining locally at a given time" should be given a "margin of appreciation" in which to exercise their discretion.[5] The Court concluded that the Austrian authorities had not overstepped the margin of appreciation.

In the juridical stew of the passages above, a number of notions are floating. It is said that the state acted to prevent offence to citizens and to ensure public order. It is said that a screening of *Das Liebeskonzil* would have infringed on the religious liberty of Catholics. Finally, it is intimated that the purveyors of the film committed a more basic failure of respect for the equal standing of persons. Each of these considerations has entered the discourse of international human rights. In Europe, the region that has developed a supranational human rights regime with the greatest degree of enforcement and compliance, the criminalization of sacrilegious expression has found favor at the highest levels.

In its ruling in Preminger and other cases, the European Court of Human Rights has strayed far beyond the universal standards of the International Bill of Rights in approving the suppression of religiously controversial expression. Particularly problematic is the Court's doctrine of the margin of appreciation, which gives national authorities broad discretion in interpreting limitations on fundamental rights. In the European context, such discretion has been tolerable because of the relative weakness of the anti-blasphemy legal regimes, where punishments are relatively mild or "proportional." But by persisting in upholding their "liberal" regimes, European human rights authorities have undermined the universality of fundamental rights of speech and conscience, contrary to the cause of human rights under illiberal regimes outside of the European context. Well before Danish and British diplomats at the United Nations began to oppose the Organisation of Islamic Cooperation's campaign against "defamation of religions," the European Court had already created a right to respect for religious feelings.

The covenant of universal human rights presupposes a moral commitment to treating persons with equal respect. Properly understood, this moral commitment to equal respect does not create a right to respect for religious belief. On the contrary, it supplies an argument for the legality of peaceful sacrilege—and most "religious hatred" and "religious defamation" as well—as a matter of principle. Despite the appalling failure to protect it fully in international discourse and law, there is a human right to blaspheme. The onus is on the agents of civil society—nongovernmental organizations, journalists, academics, educators, individual citizens—to demand that states and international bodies stand up for the free conscience even when it defiles the sacred.

Autonomy and legitimacy

Who cares if *The Council of Love* is seen? Liberals—in the classical sense—have at the ready an epistemic, or knowledge-based argument for protecting expression owing to John Stuart Mill (and his partner Harriet Taylor). Everyone, including those in power, have an interest in a free and fierce exchange of ideas because this is the best means of arriving at knowledge of the true, the right, or good, and this knowledge will enable us to flourish. Liberty conduces to knowledge. Knowledge conduces to human well-being. Hence, liberty is "the only unfailing and permanent source of improvement" to the human lot.[6]

As compelling as it is, the Millian defense of free speech leaves many anxious. It would make freedom a matter of good or interest rather than a matter of right or principle. Condorcet's Jury Theorem, a remarkable early discovery in social statistics, showed that if one wishes to decide between two options by majority vote where one of those options is correct, the probability of a correct collective choice increases with the addition of each new voter, on the assumption that the probability of each voter choosing correctly is greater than 0.5.[7] If one mind is good, more are better. Crucially, the Theorem also assumes that the voters' probabilities of correctness are independent of one another. If all voters were getting their information from the same source, for instance, then the epistemic value of each vote would be diminished. If the immediate value of speech is epistemic, a related worry attends Mill's famous dictum, "if all mankind minus one were of one opinion, and only one person were of the contrary opinion, mankind would be no more justified in silencing that one person than he, if he have the power, would be justified in silencing mankind."[8] If society has already absorbed the epistemic benefit of his contributions, why do we need to hear from him? What was there in Panizza's satire, after all, that could not be gotten from Porphyry or Paine? Accordingly, some liberals have sought a rights-based or principle-based defense of free speech that links it to the basic conditions of political legitimacy.[9]

The practice of democratic government presupposes a commitment to equal concern and respect for persons. Equal respect entails treating every person as a being capable of offering and acting in accordance with reasons, taking every person to be autonomous. Equal concern entails treating no person's reasons or interests as impartially weightier or more worthy of consideration than another's merely in virtue of who he or she is. Among possible practices of government, democratic practices are most consistent with the commitment to equal concern and respect because they most closely approximate the ideal of self-governance, or self-rule, the condition in which the reasons for the exercise of coercive power over oneself are one's own reasons, reasons that one endorses or would upon reflection endorse. To depart from the condition of self-rule, exercising coercive power over someone on the basis of reasons that are not her own is prima facie either to refuse to take her as a being capable of offering and acting in accordance with reasons or to treat her reasons as bearing less normative strength than those of another simply in virtue of who she is. Under self-government, persons are maximally autonomous, and the norms they author can be said to be autonomous rather than heteronomous: "democratic forms of government are those in which the laws are made by the same people to whom they apply (and for that reason they are autonomous norms), while in autocratic forms of government the law-makers are different from those to whom the laws are addressed (and are therefore heteronomous norms)."[10]

Perfect autonomy is impossible. In any actual human circumstance of self-rule, there will be at least two persons trying to rule themselves. And where there is more than one person, there arises the distinct possibility of irreconcilable points of view about the proper exercise of force in organizing the structure of shared life. Two autonomous beings walk into a room; three opinions emerge. Under such circumstances of actual diversity, the ideal of self-rule cannot be realized but only approximated, and this by ensuring to each person an equal opportunity to *participate in deliberations* about the structure of shared life and the terms of social cooperation. Some of these deliberations are open-ended. Some concern the nature of proper deliberation itself. Others attempt to define and circumscribe those zones within a democracy—such as the activity of self-interested, rational bargaining among politically opposed parties—where the ambit of debate is modest at best.[11] Still other deliberations come to an end without reaching a mutually agreeable resolution. In such cases, equal respect for persons is preserved to the extent that it is true, and known to be true, that the reasons of each were given a fair hearing and that the deliberative process was in some way responsive to these concerns. The rejection of one's reason by others does not constitute a lack of responsiveness, let alone disregard or disrespect, so long as the rejection is not a denial of one's equal standing. Indeed, the fact that a reason is considered and defeated testifies that its author had equal standing as a member of the moral community. Household pets and plants do not enjoy the privilege of having their proposals rejected. Even Rousseau, with his vaulting rhetoric of "the general will," did not imagine that a collective will must be unanimous to be general, but only that fair representative procedures be observed.[12]

Deliberation is more than voting. We can imagine a society in which the state "bans political parties and associations" and "proscribes public demonstrations and prohibits individuals from publishing their views to other citizens," in which each citizen must make up his or her mind in isolation.[13] If the procedures themselves are unresponsive to their ideas and interests, and if the choices presented to them on ballots have no connection to their wills, they could exercise the franchise as much as they like, and yet the results would remain heteronomous with respect to them. The voting behavior of these possible citizens is not part of a democratic practice because it does not take place within the context of a *public discourse*. Public discourse is not notional discourse. It consists in actual conversations in parliaments, political rallies, schools and universities, trade associations, print publications, radio and television broadcasts. Since public discourse is nothing but communication among persons, the freedom to form opinions and the freedom to express opinions—freedom of conscience and freedom of expression—are essential to the democratic legitimacy of the state. As Robert Post puts it:

> Democracy serves the value of self-determination by establishing a communicative structure within which the varying perspectives of individuals can be reconciled through reason. If the state were to forbid the expression of a particular idea, the government would become, with respect to individuals holding that idea, heteronomous and nondemocratic. This is incompatible with a form of government predicated upon treating its citizens "in ways consistent with their being viewed as free and equal citizens." . . . For this reason the value of self-determination requires that public discourse be open to the opinions of all.[14]

The scope of public discourse can be characterized both by its audience and by its content. Kant distinguished between the "public use of reason" and "private use of reason." While a private use of reason is directed at an audience circumscribed by some particular identity or affiliation, like a family or a religious congregation, a public use of reason is "that use which anyone may make of it as a man of learning addressing the entire reading public" or "the world at large."[15] Public discourse is about matters of concern to the public, the arrangement of the terms of shared life. John Rawls defines the domain of public reason as discussions of constitutional essentials and matters of basic justice, where constitutional essentials are the rights and liberties contained in the constitution, and matters of basic justice concern the basic structure of society: "a society's main political, social, and economic institutions, and how they fit together into one unified system of social cooperation from one generation to the next."[16] A letter to the editor in a national newspaper discussing a change in the country's immigration policy is a typical contribution to public discourse. To the extent that citizens have the opportunity to make such contributions without interference and to engage with the contributions of others, they are made more autonomous with regard to the political decisions about immigration that may follow.

This protection from interference extends even to the democratically enacted will of the majority. State protection—most robustly, in the form of constitutional protection—is necessary to save public discourse from interference by the force of majorities. If the state failed to protect minority viewpoints from majority interference, it would be failing to treat all citizens with equal respect. In public discourse, lesser publics must be protected from the greater public. And so, the very moral commitment that vindicates democratic practices—the commitment to equal respect—also shields conscience and expression from the general will of the *demos*. The freedom of conscience and the freedom of expression are not just goods that make a society better off, but conditions of a society that is morally legitimate.

In keeping with the principle that an open public discourse is a condition of democratic legitimacy, a civil libertarian approach to the regulation of speech by law, exemplified by the prevailing interpretation of the First Amendment to the US Constitution, is committed as a matter of principle to presumptive protection of speech in public discourse, a "public forum," or "'marketplace of ideas." In the First Amendment tradition, this is done by forbidding the government from engaging in content-based or viewpoint discrimination—regulating speech on the basis of the opinion, outlook or message it expresses rather than the "time, place, or manner" of its expression. In the language of First Amendment jurisprudence, a content-based restriction must pass muster under "strict scrutiny." It will be upheld only if it is necessary to further a "compelling interest" of the state and it is accomplished through the least restrictive means to further this interest.

Content-based regulation is permitted in a narrow range of cases; most importantly, defamation, the spreading of falsehood in writing (libel) or speech (slander) that injures the character or reputation of another; public nuisance that constitutes an invasion of privacy; "fighting words" whose very utterance constitutes a breach of the peace; and speech that incites or urges "imminent lawless action" and is likely to cause it. Content-based regulation may not even extend to "advocacy of the use of force or of law violation," unless the law violation is imminent and likely and the advocacy is intentional. In a nonpublic forum such as the boardroom of a commercial enterprise, however, government regulation on speech need not meet strict scrutiny. Nevertheless it must be reasonable and viewpoint-neutral.[17]

The First Amendment approach is not without difficulty, controversy, and unease. The implacable stance of the US Supreme Court on its standards of incitement and content-neutrality has often put it on the side of protecting the inflammatory, the menacing, the evil and mad. The 1969 case that produced the "imminent lawless action" standard concerned a Ku Klux Klan rally on an Ohio farm where the assembled made such contributions to public discourse as "bury the niggers" and "send the Jews back to Israel."[18] However, standards more coherent and morally defensible have yet to be discovered. This is nowhere clearer than in attempts in European national and international law to regulate sacrilegious expression. Wherever they have departed from the tests of content-neutrality and imminent lawless action, they have run afoul of the principle of political legitimacy.

Offence and public order

The court records do not reveal the name of the defendant, although they are bold enough to repeat a sample of his blasphemy. "God says that all the words are those of his messenger. Some of these words were, moreover, inspired in a surge of exultation, in Aisha's arms," Abdullah Rıza Ergüven wrote of the Prophet. "God's messenger broke his fast through sexual intercourse, after dinner and before prayer. Muhammad did not forbid sexual intercourse with a dead person or a living animal."[19] *Yasak Tümceler*, or *The Forbidden Phrases*, a novel of ideas by Ergüven, was published in Turkey in 1993 with a modest print run of 2,000. The managing director of the publisher, known in the records as "I. A.," was prosecuted under Article 175 sections 3 and 4 of the Criminal Code for publishing blasphemies against "God, the Religion, the Prophet and the Holy Book." In May 1996 the Istanbul Court of First Instance sentenced him to 2 years' imprisonment, later commuting this to a fine.

In September 2005 the Strasbourg Court found that Turkey's interference with the publisher's rights had been prescribed by law and had "pursued the legitimate aims of preventing disorder and protecting morals and the rights of others."[20] The seven judges were divided on whether the interference had been "necessary in a democratic society." They saw themselves as "weighing up the conflicting interests relating to the exercise of two fundamental freedoms, namely the applicant's right to impart his ideas on religious theory to the public, on the one hand, and the right of others to respect for their freedom of thought, conscience and religion, on the other hand."[21]

The Court narrowly decided that Turkey had not violated I.A.'s rights, and this because "the present case concerned not only comments that were disturbing or shocking or a 'provocative' opinion but an abusive attack on the Prophet of Islam."

> Notwithstanding the fact that there was a certain tolerance of criticism of religious doctrine within Turkish society, which is deeply attached to the principle of secularity, believers may legitimately feel themselves to be the

object of unwarranted and offensive attacks. . . . The Court therefore considers that the measure taken . . . was intended to provide protection against offensive attacks on matters regarded as sacred by Muslims. In that respect it finds that the measure may reasonably be held to have met a "pressing social need."[22]

In reaching this decision, the Court took into account the fact that the Turkish courts had not decided to seize the book in question, and consequently held that the insignificant fine imposed had been "proportionate" to the aims pursued by the measure.[23]

Is the Court's "right to respect" the right not to be offended, grounded in the Convention principle of public disorder? Public disorder is one of the permissible grounds for limiting expression laid out in Article 10:

Article 10

1. Everyone has the right to freedom of expression. This right shall include freedom to hold opinions and to receive and impart information and ideas without interference by public authority and regardless of frontiers. This article shall not prevent States from requiring the licensing of broadcasting, television or cinema enterprises.

2. The exercise of these freedoms, since it carries with it duties and responsibilities, may be subject to such formalities, conditions, restrictions or penalties as are prescribed by law and are necessary in a democratic society, in the interests of national security, territorial integrity or public safety, for the prevention of disorder or crime, for the protection of health or morals, for the protection of the reputation or the rights of others, for preventing the disclosure of information received in confidence, or for maintaining the authority and impartiality of the judiciary.

The judgment against the Otto-Preminger-Institut, like the judgment against Panizzi in Munich, did not find an injury to God, Jesus, or Mary, least of all Satan, who comes out of the play with his reputation intact. It found an affront to their followers. In Wingrove v. United Kingdom, the Court upheld a decision by the British Board of Film Classification to deny a certificate to *Visions of Ecstasy*, a short film that depicts the sixteenth-century Carmelite nun St. Teresa of Avila becoming a little too reverent with the supine body of the crucified Christ. According to the Court, the Board acted legitimately to protect against "seriously offensive attacks on matters regarded as sacred by Christians."[24] In *Murphy v. Ireland*, the Court allowed to stand a ban on an advertisement on commercial radio by the Irish Faith Centre, a small evangelical organization based in Dublin, for the reason that "the religious advertising coming from a different church can be offensive to many people."[25]

The United Kingdom's venerable public order tradition is also still used to address the problem of religiously provocative expression. Three hundred and twenty five years after John Taylor caused a scene by calling Christ a whoremonger, a preacher named Harry John Hammond drew a jeering, belligerent crowd in the town square of Bournemouth. This time, in twenty-first century secular Britain, it was not an expression of sacrilegious anti-Christianity but the profession of evangelical Christianity that drew an unruly mob. Hammond was displaying placards reading, "Stop Immorality," "Stop Homosexuality," and "Stop Lesbianism." In the course of the confrontation, some in the crowd of several dozen threw soil at him, doused him with water and snatched away his sign, causing him to fall to the ground. Yet it was Hammond who was arrested for "provoking violence" in breach of the peace. He was convicted under the Public Order Act of 1986.[26]

Absent a real danger of the wrath of Sappho raining down on Bournemouth, why should the disorderly conduct be blamed on Hammond instead of his hecklers? Perhaps it could be blamed on him if he had incited the violence. Indeed, the court ruled that Hammond's words went "beyond legitimate protest" because they were "insulting"; they "caused distress" and "interfered with the rights of others." Here the public order rationale is met with a dilemma. Does the insult or provocation owe to the *matter* being presented or to the *manner* of its presentation, to the cognitive meaning of the act or to its character as a social behavior? Is the blasphemer the provocateur because of what he says or the way he says it? If the latter, then the legal threshold for blasphemous disorder would be set far higher than mere contradiction of the opinion prevalent among mob or magistrate. Had Hammond's manner and conduct been identical but his sign replaced with "Start Lesbianism"—or, for that matter, "Christ is a whoremonger"—the worldly onlookers most likely would have passed him by without a stir.[27]

If instead insult is determined by the content of the expression, such as the gravity of its transgression of prevailing opinion, then who is to make those content-based determinations? Should the culpability for causing a public disorder be brought into existence by the judgment of legal authorities? And to whom falls the prior determination of which kind of insult is relevant? In the case of Hammond, the appeals court held that it was "open to the justices" to determine which expressions could be considered insulting within the meaning of the Act.[28] This would appear to make the religiously heterodox hostage to the pro-clivities of those elites with the power to stipulate contestable social norms of public morality and decency. The centuries in between Taylor and Hammond had so inverted public morality that it was the pious Christian who took on the role of dissenter and the "tolerant" pluralists who communally rose up in spontaneous intimidation and violence to secure secular orthodoxy.

The appeal to offence would be over and done with if offence of any kind were never sufficient grounds for the intervention of coercive law. "Liberty consists in the freedom to do everything which injures no one else," says the Declaration of the Rights of Man, leaving open what counts as injury. A strict interpretation of injury can be found in Mill's oft-touted, seldom-comprehended Liberty Principle, or Harm Principle, which says that "the sole end for which mankind are warranted, individually or collectively, in interfering with the liberty of action of any of their number, is self-protection. That the only purpose for which power can be rightfully exercised over any member of a civilized community, against his will, is to prevent harm to others." Two paragraphs later, Mill explains that a harm entails the frustration of an individual's rights or interests—"permanent interests of man as a progressive being."[29] This would seem to distinguish harm from offence. A harm is a set-back to one's interests. An offence is an intrinsically unpleasant experience that does not in itself frustrate any of a person's important interests, apart from, of course, a general interest in not having unpleasant experiences. Offence lives in subjectivity. While you can be harmed without being aware of the harm—someone secretly poisons your friends against you—to be offended you must be aware of the offending state of affairs.

Anglo-American law already provides for a category of criminal and civil wrongdoing that falls short of harm: nuisance. The philosopher Joel Feinberg has argued that the Harm Principle must be supplemented by the Offence Principle, and he builds his analysis on the model of civil and criminal laws against nuisances: "a landowner can sue his neighbor for private nuisance when the latter keeps a howling dog (irritating others) . . . whereas an intentional or negligent wrongdoer can be convicted of 'public nuisance' in a criminal court for unreasonably obstructing a public highway (inconveniencing others)," "holding indecent public exhibitions (shocking others)," or "conducting cock fights or dog fights (offending the sensibilities of others)."[30] Anyone who has ever ridden New York City public transportation on New Year's Eve knows that there are non-harmful behaviors that beg for legal regulation.[31] That colorfully condensed harm principle of US Supreme Court Justice Oliver Wendell Holmes, "The right to swing my fist ends where the other man's nose begins," fails to consider the foulness that might be going on under my nose.

Offending conduct, says Feinberg, "produces unpleasant or uncomfortable experiences—affronts to the sense or sensibility, disgust, shock, shame, embarrassment, annoyance, boredom, anger, fear, or humiliation—from which one cannot escape without unreasonable inconvenience or even harm." We are moved to seek legal remedy for nuisances "when we think of ourselves as trapped by them, and we think it unfair that we should pay the cost in inconvenience that is required to escape them."[32] The Offence Principle holds that it is "always a good reason in support of a proposed criminal prohibition that it is probably necessary to prevent serious offence to persons other than the actor and would probably be an effective means to that end if enacted."[33]

Offensiveness is not a brute fact. Neither is it the only consideration. There are other considerations to be weighed in the balance by a
responsible legislator, which may defeat the reason generated by offensiveness. The seriousness of an offence, says Feinberg, is determined
by three criteria. There is the matter of reasonable *inescapability*:
"the ease with which unwilling witnesses can avoid the offensive
displays." There is the principle of *Volenti non fit injuria*—to a willing person, no injury is done: Is it the case that "the witnesses have
willingly assumed the risk of being offended either through curiosity
or the anticipation of pleasure"? Third, there is *extent*: "the intensity
and durability of the repugnance produced, and the extent to which
repugnance could be anticipated to be the general reaction of strangers to the conduct displayed or represented (conduct offensive only
to persons with an abnormal susceptibility to offence would not count
as very offensive)."[34] Sensitivity to disgust, shock, shame, embarrassment, annoyance, boredom, anger, fear, or humiliation make possible
a claim of offence. But certain kinds of oversensitivity will render such
a claim unwarranted. It will not do to think of "abnormal susceptibility" to offence in a strictly empirical or statistical sense. For some
susceptibilities to offence are not just unusual, but unreasonable or
morally objectionable. The racist whose blood is boiled by the sight of
an interracial couple is not just suffering from a statistically abnormal
susceptibility. No matter how widespread the susceptibility might be,
we should still want to say that this experience of offence does not
count as a reason for prohibiting interracial coupling.[35]

Along with the extent, inescapability, and voluntariness of the experience of offence, one must consider the reasonableness of the conduct
that produced it; that is, the *importance* of the conduct to the actor
or others, the *availability* of alternative times and places and modes
of expression that would produce less offence, and the *motive* of the
offending conduct. Depending on how these conditions are fulfilled,
a case of offence could be wrongful or not wrongful. My irritation,
caused by my neighbor's noise, even if it is against my will, inescapable, severe and not a product of peculiarly sensitive ears, might not
be wrongful if my neighbor is an airport that is serving an important

public function which could not be performed in a less noisy and noisome way.

How does blasphemy fare on this model of offence? What of the European Court's assertion of a right of citizens not to be "insulted in their religious feelings"? Clearly, the alleged victims of I. A.'s publication fail the condition of inescapability. *The Forbidden Phrases* did not invade the consciousness of anyone who did not invite them. In fact, the publicity surrounding the case may have assisted them in avoiding it. It could be argued that some Muslims suffered an affront to their religious sensibilities from the *bare knowledge* that the book was being read, even if they were not reading it. Feinberg calls this "profound offence." No doubt, this kind of shock to the sensibilities can be real and no less disturbing than an assault on the senses. Profound offence is a puzzle. For, to be a proper subject of the law, it needs a victim, someone who has been wronged. But nothing permits us to say of any particular Turkish citizen that something was *done to her* by the blasphemous content. Wouldn't it be more plausible to say that the victim was the Prophet?

Furthermore, *The Forbidden Phrases* made a contribution to public discourse. To be sure, superficially the work connected a revered religious figure with unsavory sexuality. But as a comment on the nature of Islamic faith, the book had implications for the basic structure of Turkish society. And as a public use of reason, the book was participating in the processes of social communication whose freedom is a precondition for the legitimacy of state power. The law that forbade the author's phrases from entering public discourse made the state less responsive to his views and made less legitimate the state's policies on which they bear. This constituted a failure of respect for autonomy.[36] The same cannot be said of the unnamed, alleged victims of Ergüven's "offensive attack," the totality of "believers" and "Muslims" on Turkey's territory as the Court would have it. Those who took profound offence at the work were not thereby been treated with less respect than their unperturbed neighbors. For the policies that permitted the circulation of *The Forbidden Phrases* were not calibrated to offend them, denigrate their concerns, or deny their autonomy, but rather to create and sustain social practices of communication that would enable their own views to be heard and registered in public opinion. The European Court was correct that the conditions for democracy were at stake in I. A. v Turkey. Contrary to its judgment, it was not the overbroad Article 175 of Turkey's Criminal Code that was "necessary to a democratic society," but *The Forbidden Phrases*.

The rights of others

The right to respect for religious beliefs cries out for some kind of derivation from more general Convention principles. One possibility is Article 9's protection of freedom of religion or belief:

Article 9

1. Everyone has the right to freedom of thought, conscience and religion; this right includes freedom to change his religion or belief, and freedom, either alone or in community with others and in public or private, to manifest his religion or belief in worship, teaching, practice and observance.

2. Freedom to manifest one's religion or beliefs shall be subject only to such limitations as are prescribed by law and are necessary in a democratic society in the interests of public safety, for the protection of public order, health or morals, or the protection of the rights and freedoms of others.

Though the history of its drafting was quite different, this article corresponds to the ICCPR guarantee of freedom of religion or belief in Article 18.

The Preminger judgment asserts that desecration of beliefs "can be such as to inhibit those who hold such beliefs from exercising their freedom to hold and express them." The idea here is that expressive abuse of one's belief can make it significantly difficult to manifest that belief in religious practice. As an empirical hypothesis, this is bold to say the least. Is it in fact the case that Catholics are made less free by the existence of blasphemous movies? Here as with so many other blasphemies, the perpetrator was vulnerable to criminal prosecution precisely because his speech or practice was out of step with the march of a more powerful majority. The thought that it is the majority audience and not the blasphemer whose liberties are in peril is on its face, preposterous. And yet, the Court adduced no evidence in support of this claim in this case. Meanwhile, decisions in other cases cut against it.

In Choudhury v. United Kingdom, the Court held that states are not obligated to introduce blasphemy laws in order to protect citizens' right to manifest their religion or belief.[37] In Kokkinakis v. Greece, it affirmed the value of pluralism and religious dissent:

> As enshrined in Article 9, freedom of thought, conscience and religion is one of the foundations of a "democratic society" within the meaning of the Convention. It is, in its religious dimension, one of the most vital elements that go to make up the identity of believers and their conception of life, but it is also a precious asset for atheists, agnostics, skeptics and the unconcerned. The pluralism indissociable from a democratic society, which has been dearly won over the centuries, depends on it.[38]

The Court found that the right of a Jehovah's Witness to manifest his religion or belief entailed the right to try to persuade his neighbors on religious matters. The free interplay of ideas on religious matters may include criticism and even hostility. The Preminger opinion noted that in a pluralistic society, believers "must tolerate and accept the denial by others of their religious beliefs and even the propagation by others of doctrines hostile to their faith."[39] If any rejection of a religious practice were sufficient to violate the freedom of those who adhere to it, then every religion would impinge on that freedom, for every religion rejects some practice of its alternatives—or else they would not be alternatives at all. If this were what freedom of conscience meant, it could only be preserved by absolute unanimity or absolute silence. If, contrary to the facts of Preminger, blasphemous speech were somehow sufficient to create a pervasive atmosphere of hostility and intimidation, then believers might be victims of "religious hatred," a possibility considered below.

If the "right to respect" for a belief is not a right to be free from insult or offence, or a right to the manifestation of that belief, then what is it? It appears that the Strasbourg officials are asserting a *sui generis* right not recognized at the universal level of United Nations standards, including the ICCPR.[40] In doing so, they have breached universal human rights standards in elaborating an overly broad understanding of the "rights of others."

In I. A. v. Turkey, we are met with the extraordinary spectacle of a human rights court in Strasbourg recognizing the religious crime of impugning the honor of the Prophet, something Turkey's own legal reforms later removed from its statutes.[41] How was this possible? Here is a hypothesis. Had the Court located such a law within the categories of European experience with communal blasphemy and spiritual blasphemy, the law would have been classified as an enemy of the secular principles of pluralism and separation of powers.[42] Instead, it located the law within the categories of personal blasphemy, under the standard of respect for persons. This banner of "respect" was wide enough to gather up both the recognition respect presupposed by human rights norms and the respect for honor at work in *sabb*, the moral assumptions of which are incompatible with recognition respect. A theocratic conceit could appear at home next to the law of insult, particularly deeply rooted in France and in Germany, where the elastic *Achtung* forms its conceptual core.[43] An illiberal concept of respect was assimilated to a liberal concept of respect, as an "abusive attack" on the Prophet was equated with an "offensive attack" on the dignity of his followers.

Religious hatred

By 2008, the debate on blasphemy at the United Nations had begun shifting away from talk of "defamation of religions" to talk of "advocacy of religious hatred," or hate speech.[44] By equating sacrilegious speech with religious hate speech, its opponents could avail themselves of a well-established international norm. For Article 20(2) of the ICCPR already imposes a restriction on freedom of expression by prohibiting "advocacy of national, racial or religious hatred that constitutes incitement to discrimination, hostility or violence." The International Convention on the Elimination of All Forms of Racial Discrimination calls for bans on speech that attempts "to justify or promote racial hatred or discrimination in any form." The United States is anomalous in its constitutional guarantee of free speech, which has been interpreted to extend to hate speech. The US has ratified the international treaties with the "reservation" that they cannot contravene First Amendment protections. Meanwhile, almost every Council of Europe member state outlaws hate speech; roughly half outlaw "religious insult."[45]

Seen from some philosophical remove, it might appear that a blatant mistake is being made in the attempt to treat blasphemous satire, profanity, or indecorum with such legal instruments, designed as they are for dealing with wrongs to persons or groups rather than deities, sacred objects, or texts. It may seem obvious that one can abuse an icon without thereby abusing those who venerate it, and defame a Prophet without thereby defaming those who follow him. If so, then blasphemy could be distinguished in principle from religious hate speech. Whatever the philosophical attractions of such a view, if you descend to the scale of specific laws and cases, the scene changes.

Consider the recent attempts by the United Kingdom to address religious hatred within the public order tradition. Since the late Victorian dust-up over *The Freethinker*, convictions for blasphemous libel had dwindled, though they enjoyed a recrudescence in the scandalous 1977 *Gay News* case. The country repealed its common law offences of blasphemy and blasphemous libel in 2008 after coming under mounting criticism for discrimination against non-Christians since the law singled out one faith for protection. In multicultural Britain, the law had come to be seen as an emblem of cultural chauvinism, targeting as it did communal blasphemy, the blasphemy against one particular community.[46] With it, the "part and parcel" doctrine, entrenched in common law since the 1675 blasphemy decision against John Taylor, was at last cast away.

The Racial and Religious Hatred Act of 2006, an amendment to the Public Order Act of 1986, was passed following on a public campaign to give to Muslims the same kind of protection on religious grounds that was already being granted to Sikhs and Jews as "racial" groups under the existing Act. It created criminal offences of "stirring up hatred against persons on religious grounds." Finalized in the midst of vociferous protests by writers and performers including Salman Rushdie and the comedian Rowan Atkinson, the Act included a provision to reinforce freedom of expression: "Nothing in the Part shall be read or given effect in a way which prohibits or restricts discussion, criticism or expressions of antipathy, dislike, ridicule, insult or abuse of particular religions or the beliefs or practices of their adherents, or of any other belief system or the beliefs or practices of its adherents, or proselytizing or urging adherents of a different religion or belief system to cease practicing their religion or belief system."[47]

The Religious Hatred Act is relatively narrowly construed. After considering but rejecting an earlier draft of the law, which would have criminalized behavior that was considered *abusive* or *insulting*, the House of Commons accepted a final version that criminalized only "threatening words or behaviour" intended to stir up hatred. Still, British authorities have at their disposal other public order instruments that give them far greater latitude, including Anti-Social Behaviour Orders; the Public Order Act's prohibition of "abusive" and "insulting" statements likely to cause "harassment, alarm, or distress";[48] and "religiously aggravated" offences—in accordance with the Crime and Disorder Act of 1998, which provides for higher maximum penalties for certain crimes "motivated (wholly or partly) by hostility towards members of a racial or religious group based on their membership of that group."[49]

A teenage boy arrived at a peaceful demonstration against the Church of Scientology on a sidewalk outside of the church's London headquarters on 10 May 2008. He had brought along a sign reading, "Scientology is not a religion, it is a dangerous cult." The boy was informed by the police that he was not allowed to use the word "cult," and was "strongly advised" to stop displaying the sign or face charges under section 5 of the Public Order Act for making insulting and abusive statements. He refused, citing a high court judgment from 1984 in which Scientology was described with the "c" word. The police confiscated his sign and issued a summons.[50] Later that month, the Crown Prosecution Service ruled that the word was neither abusive nor insulting, and the boy would face no prosecution.

In early 2010, an atheist named Harry Taylor walked into a public prayer chapel at Liverpool John Lennon Airport and left behind leaflets bearing three anti-religious cartoons. One "depicted a smiling crucified Christ next to an advert for a brand of 'no nails' glue. In another, a cartoon depicted two Muslims holding a placard demanding equality with the caption: 'Not for women or gays, obviously.' A third poster showed Islamic suicide bombers at the gates of paradise being told: 'Stop, stop, we've run out of virgins.'"[51] He was convicted of "religiously aggravated harassment" and sentenced to a 6-month suspended sentence and an Anti-Social Behaviour Order barring him from carrying anti-religious materials in public.

These stories are instructive about how tempting it can be, within a public order framework, to collapse provocative religious criticism with hostility toward the members of a religious community. What would make such public order restrictions on speech morally legitimate? The speech could be fighting words with which one forgoes communication and initiates actual combat beginning with verbal blows, or it could be incitement to imminent lawless action. If so, then the wrongfulness of the speech owes not to its objectionable content, but to its character as an action—a provocation or incitement, and a legal instrument targeting "abusive" or "insulting" speech would be targeting the wrong thing. Alternatively, the wrongfulness of the speech could be located in the feelings of offence or alarm caused. If so, then the case for policing hate speech reduces to the case for policing offensive or harassing speech, which is subject to the serious limitations noted above, especially the condition of *inescapability*: How inescapable is a leaflet in a Liverpool prayer room?

Finally, the wrongfulness could be located in the emotion of hostility in the speaker. Even if Harry Taylor had been motivated by hostility toward Christians and Muslims, would this have made him a proper subject of legal sanction? Why should an expression of hostility to a religious community be illegal? After all, there is nothing intrinsically evil about hatred, nothing necessarily abhorrent in abhorrence. Walt Whitman exhorts us to resist much, obey little, and "hate tyrants." What is abhorrent in a democratic society is rather the treatment of some citizens as intrinsically inferior and subordinate. As noted in Kokkinakis v. Greece, one person's exercise of his freedom of conscience may be experienced by another as hostility. As an atheist, Taylor had a fundamental right to exercise this freedom, even if it were to engender hostility toward the faithful. By contrast, no one has the right to a world in which he is never despised. Taylor also had the right to participate in the processes of democratic deliberation about the place of religion in society. By barring Taylor from participating fully in public discourse, the government violated his autonomy and acted illegitimately. By permitting a skeptic to voice his hostility, by contrast, the state is not treating the believer with less concern or respect since it is not thereby endorsing the skeptic's skepticism.

In the case of Norwood v. United Kingdom, the conflict between freedom of expression and public order restrictions was brought before the European Court of Human Rights, which found something else wrong in religious hate speech. The case concerned Mark Anthony Norwood, a regional organizer for the right-wing British National Party who in the winter of 2001 displayed a BNP-produced sign in his window bearing the words "Islam out of Britain—Protect the British People" along with an image of the Twin Towers ablaze and a crescent and star in a prohibition symbol.[52] The sign was confiscated and its owner charged with religiously aggravated display of a threatening, abusive or insulting representation. In rejecting Norwood's claim that the British government had violated his freedom of expression, the Court relied on a precedent concerning Article 17 of the Convention, the so-called abuse clause, which states, "Nothing in [the] Convention may be interpreted as implying for any State, group or person any right to engage in any activity or perform any act aimed at the destruction of any of the rights and freedoms

set forth herein or at their limitation to a greater extent than is provided for in the Convention." According to this precedent, freedom
of expression "may not be invoked in a sense contrary to Article 17."[53]
But Norwood's expression, the decision concluded, did just this. His
"vehement attack against a religious group, linking the group as a
whole with a grave act of terrorism, is incompatible with the values
proclaimed and guaranteed by the Convention, notably tolerance,
social peace and non-discrimination."

While nowhere near thoughtful or constructive, Norwood's speech
nevertheless was an entry into public deliberation on matters of great
public concern in British society: the ideology of multiculturalism,
immigration and anti-terrorism policy, and the status of *sharia* law
within the country. Since the speech fell well short of incitement to
imminent unlawful behavior—actual employment discrimination, for
instance—the question of whether or not his implicit opinions were
"aimed at the destruction" of norms of tolerance, peace, or "non-discrimination" is itself part of matter under public deliberation. Mark
Anthony Norwood may have been mistaken that Islamist ideology
could be driven out of Britain without massive violation of people's
rights. Yet a government that prevents democratic processes from
being receptive to his reasoning, that denies him the opportunity to be
mistaken publicly, has diminished the legitimacy of those of its policies on which his beliefs bear.

Perhaps what is troubling about cultural xenophobia like Norwood's
is not an attitude of animosity, or even a challenge to establishment
understandings of toleration and egalitarianism, but an outright denial
of equal standing to some citizens. Perhaps what crosses the line from
protected to unprotected speech is not the defamation of religions but
the defamation of the religious.

Group defamation

The French novelist Michel Houellebecq wound up in court for
describing Islam in an interview with a literary magazine as "the

dumbest" of all religions (in fairness, Houellebecq came out against all monotheistic faiths, but found Islam's sacred text especially wanting: "In literary terms, the Bible has several authors, some good and some as bad as crap. The Koran has only one author and its overall style is mediocre").[54] Charges were brought by mosques in Paris and Lyon, the National Federation of French Muslims, the World Islamic League, and the Human Rights League. Representing the plaintiffs, the prominent Algerian-born French Muslim Dalil Boubaker told the court: "Islam has been reviled, attacked with hateful words. My community has been humiliated."

French law designates six group identities—race, ethnicity, gender, sexual orientation, religious belief, and disability—and attempts by law to protect them against three types of offences set out in the 1881 Law on the Freedom of the Press: "abuse," "defamation," and "provocation to discrimination."[55] Abuse is understood to be "any offensive expression, term of contempt, or invective that does not impute any fact" and a defamation is understood to be "any allegation or imputation of a fact that damages the honor of or consideration for the person or group to whom the fact is imputed." Though Houellebecq was eventually acquitted, the case illustrates how a ready legal recourse against religious abuse and defamation can invite accusations that obscure the difference between contempt for a text and contempt for a community, and slip from "Islam has been reviled" to "my community has been humiliated."

In another French case, the historian and writer Paul Giniewski was convicted of religious defamation for "The Obscurity of Error," an article he published in a Paris newspaper criticizing Pope John Paul II's encyclical, *The Splendour of Truth*. "The Catholic Church institutes itself as the sole guardian of divine truth," Giniewski wrote. "It loudly proclaims the fulfilment of the Old Covenant in the New, the superiority of the latter. . . . Many Christians have recognized that scriptural anti-Judaism and the doctrine of 'fulfilment' of the Old Covenant in the New led to anti-Semitism and prepared the ground in which the idea and implementation of Auschwitz took seed."[56] The judge in the initial conviction believed that Giniewski's assertion was "evidently damaging to the honor of and consideration for Christians and particularly for the Catholic community." While the defendant was "within his rights to denounce Christian anti-Semitism in history and to warn readers against any new manifestation or resurgence of this sentiment," nothing "gave him the authority to use extreme terms upon the release of the Pope's new encyclical reasserting the doctrine of 'fulfilment' and, by means of confusions, to attribute responsibility for the Nazi massacres committed at Auschwitz to the Catholic community."

In their readings of "The Obscurity of Error," French judges showed their willingness to embrace such a broad conception of religious defamation as to encompass even sober historical disputation about doctrine. Nevertheless, the French cases embody the model of hate speech—distinct from the public disorder model—that claims a number of distinguished theoreticians as defenders as well as a hegemonic hold across much of Europe: the model of hate speech as *group defamation*.[57] If extreme religious expression in practice cannot be extricated from hate speech in European and international law, what can be said about these hate speech laws?[58]

They cannot simply be dismissed as illiberal or undemocratic. Even many strict civil libertarians admit that defamation against individuals is unprotected speech on the grounds that state interference in defamatory speech does not rob the marketplace of ideas of any epistemic value or violate the speaker's fundamental right of democratic participation in the formation of public opinion because malicious falsehoods have no proper place in the formation of public opinion. It might be thought that if this reasoning holds for individual libel and slander, it should hold for libel and slander against groups as well.[59] From the perspective of a liberal theory of political legitimacy founded on the equal standing of citizens, there is an even stronger case for outlawing group defamation.

Like the rights-based or equality-based argument for freedom of speech, a rights-based or equality-based argument for legal protection against hate speech begins with the commitment to according equal standing to all persons, showing them equal recognition respect. However, it finds that political legitimacy is not only conditional on the state treating persons equally. The state must also ensure that *persons* treat each other equally. "Although individuals have a right to take part in public discourse, they also have a duty to respect other citizens as equal participants in that discourse. In other words, it is not enough that the state should view individuals as free and equal; citizens must also view one another in this light."[60] The denigration of a group—at the limit, the descriptions of members of the targeted groups as animals or vermin—constitutes a denial by some persons of equal standing to others.[61] The condition of political legitimacy is not simply the existence of a public discourse in which all are free, but a public discourse in which all participants grant equal standing to each other. Therefore, by intervening to prevent hate speech, the state is not violating but ensuring the conditions of legitimacy.

Note that the equality-based argument for regulation of hate speech need not suppose that groups are independent entities—apart from all of the individuals that make them up—that can somehow suffer wrongs in their own right. Instead, in the final moral analysis, what matters is the equality of individuals. Nor is an equality-based theory of group defamation based on a *feeling* of offence or affront experienced by the targeted group. The standing of a person could be assaulted without her knowing it. Further, such a theory can set aside the question of hatred, understood as an extreme emotion of negative animus. It focuses not on what perpetrators feel but on what they *do*—their speech acts of subordination. Defamation is "a special kind of discriminatory practice, a verbal form inequality takes."[62]

This argument, or something like it, establishes a moral requirement on citizens to treat their fellows as equals, to "act towards one another in a spirit of brotherhood," in the Universal Declaration's phrase. But it fails to show that the state legitimately may intervene to ensure this. When the state intervenes to protect an individual from a defamatory attack on his basic standing as an equal member of the moral community, the beneficiary of this intervention is clear and uncontested. However, were the state to intervene to protect a *group* from denigration, the beneficiary would be neither clear nor uncontested. The six categories protected in French law—race, ethnicity, gender, sexual orientation, religious belief, and disability—are not biological categories or natural kinds but social identities that are open to moral contestation and renegotiation in public discourse.[63]

If you say of any one Catholic that she believes the New Covenant to be superior to the Old, the warrant for your statement could in principle be established through confirmation of matters of fact about that person. But if you say that *Catholics* believe the New Covenant to be superior to the Old, the warrant for that statement is more than just a matter of fact. Some Catholics will believe it, and some will not. The question of whether the statement is warranted is a question of how Catholicism is most appropriately characterized. And that question is inherently normative. It would not do to conduct a public opinion survey and generalize from the position of the majority of Catholics, for one might reasonably think that the majority of Catholics at any given time could be mistaken about the *best* interpretation of the faith.

It is often the purported *victims* of hate speech who have the most interest in contesting the social identities that the state would accept as the basis for action against group defamation. When Boubaker told the court that *his* community had been humiliated, which community did he mean—the community of French Muslims, foreign-born French Muslims, European Muslims, or perhaps the entire *umma*? These are not idle questions, but central matters of intense, sometimes life-or-death controversy over what it means to be a Muslim. Is a Muslim one who follows the five pillars of Islam, or one who lives by *shari'a*? What of those secular citizens born to Muslim parents—were they members of Boubaker's community? Or those devout citizens who believed that the Quran is not the literal, inerrant word of God, or that Islam did not need help from the force of the Republic's laws to be defended from the musings of a novelist provocateur?

The problem of contestable group identity cannot be resolved by recourse to the surface grammar, as it were, by taking at face value the group labels. Many defamations will not mention any group by name, but leave the connection to be drawn by the reader, or, in the case of cartoons, will literally draw a connection to be interpreted by the viewer. And of course, even the group titles in common currency can be subject to intense public controversy. Consider the debate over the proper appellation for a jihadi terrorist: Muslim, conservative Muslim, Islamic fundamentalist, Islamist, Islamofascist, and so on. Indeed, not even the ascription "jihadi" is religiously neutral and purely factual.

For purposes of directing coercive law, no democratic majority, boisterous minority, or administrative elite has the right to tell all of these various citizens which of these various meanings of Muslim identity or Catholic identity is more "real" or "authentic." But by intervening on behalf of the standing of "Muslims" or "Catholics," the state cannot avoid throwing its weight behind some conception of these social identities to the exclusion of others. These competing conceptions touch on questions of constitutional essentials and the basic structure of society—such as questions of whether *sharia* law or Vatican power are fully compatible with a secular liberal society. As a matter of basic democratic political legitimacy, such questions must be left to free deliberation in public discourse. Therefore, as a matter of basic democratic political legitimacy, the state may not intervene to suppress group defamatory hate speech.

But aren't there some issues—such as the equal basic standing of all racial groups—which have been so settled in political life as to leave nothing morally respectable to deliberate about? It is not as though we must suspend judgment on racial equality until the last bigot has spoken. Whether or not this analysis holds in the case of race, I maintain that it fails in the case of religion. For ideas about religion surely bear on open questions of public interest, not the least of which is the question of the proper relationship of religion to politics.

It might be responded further that the problem of contestable group identity has no bearing on cases of hate speech where there is no substantive claim or matter or fact, where someone is called vermin or scum. The contested politics of group identity, it seems, could not prevent us from banning hate speech that is not tied to any purported group characteristic; speech that is pure denigration or abuse. For in such cases there would be no purported characteristic of the target group over which public opinion could divide. Since *no* persons, whatever their group membership, are vermin or scum, we can make a determination of denigration without attaching any contested content to a group identity.

Plot religiously controversial speech on a line with pure denigration of religious believers at point Alpha and pure desecration of the divine at point Omega. Whatever you may want to say about Alpha, it is clear that if you locate an expression there, that expression is not blasphemy in that it will have nothing whatever to do with the abuse of the divine or the transgression of approved spiritual practice. To depart Alpha and move in the direction of Omega, you must add some substance to the expression beyond the mere denial of equal moral standing to religious believers—as in the remark by the right-wing British politician Nick Griffin that Islam is "a vicious, wicked faith." Yet once this content is in place, any attempt to determine for the purposes of law whether the reputation or standing of a group has been impugned will have to attribute some characteristics to the group, thus illegitimately interfering in public deliberation about the substance of contested religious identities. So, in cases where "religious hatred" is pure abuse of believers, it escapes the above argument. But it is not sensibly considered blasphemy. Where "religious hatred" is blasphemy, legal regulation will be illegitimate.

Even the legal case for the regulation of pure hate speech faces a grave challenge on empirical or pragmatic grounds. The pragmatic case against hate speech laws is built on the empirical hypothesis that such laws cannot effectively combat hate and may make it worse. For Millian reasons, it might be supposed that the best way to combat hateful speech is by exposing it to public scrutiny through legal public discourse, whereas "forcing hate speech underground obscures the extent and location of the problem to which society must respond."[64] This worry is particularly acute in an internet age, in which millions of online undergrounds provide echo-chambers for anonymous extremists. It could also be thought that suppression of hate speech is likely to radicalize the hateful, to inflame extremists' "sense of oppression and their willingness to express their views violently" and undermine the democratic practice of conflict resolution through reconciliation by public reason rather than coercion and force. Criminalization and prosecution of hate speech is likely to "divert political energies away from more effective and meaningful responses, especially those directed at changing material conditions in which racism festers." Finally, "the principle justifying prohibitions and the specific laws prohibiting hate speech are likely to be abused, creating a slippery slope to results contrary to the needs of victims of racial hatred . . . and to the needs of other marginalized groups." While the histories of entire societies are anything but controlled experiments, the experiences of western European states—where anti-Semitism, racism, and xenophobia are all alive and well—are certainly consistent with the hypothesis that legislation is not an effective means to deal with hatred.

The right to blaspheme

Like all human rights instruments, the European Convention includes in a nondiscrimination norm (corresponding to ICCPR Article 26) that guarantees equality in the enjoyment of all the rights it sets forward.

Article 14

1. All persons are equal before the law and are entitled without any discrimination to the equal protection of the law. In this respect, the law shall prohibit any discrimination and guarantee to all persons equal and effective protection against discrimination on any ground such as race, colour, sex, language, religion, political or other opinion, national or social origin, property, birth or other status.

2. The enjoyment of the rights and freedoms set forth in this Convention shall be secured without discrimination on any ground such as sex, race, colour, language, religion, political or other opinion, national or social origin, association with a national minority, property, birth or other status.

The nondiscrimination norm has two implications. First, laws against blasphemy, religious insult, and religious defamation are inherently discriminatory insofar as they provide a legal recourse to the adherents of traditional faiths that is not available to those of unrecognized faiths or secular persuasions. Second, the international legal right of freedom of thought, conscience and religion must be extended to cover the religiously offensive expressions of the religiously heterodox and secular.

According to the authoritative opinion of the Human Rights Committee, the body of 18 "independent experts" who are mandated to monitor compliance with the ICCPR by the parties to the treaty, "[p]rohibitions of displays of lack of respect for a religion or other belief system, including blasphemy laws, are incompatible with the Covenant "when they" discriminate in favor of or against one or certain religions or belief systems, or their adherents over another, or religious believers over non-believers."[65] If the state is to treat persons as equals, it cannot say that B. R. Ambedkar's attitudes toward the sacred are not candidates for legal protection just because they are not associated with what is called a "religion" by anthropological consensus.

Blasphemy can be the expression, if only implicit, of stances toward things spiritual. It can also be part of a spiritual practice. At its best, religious practice is a manifestation of the human search for answers to ultimate questions—the nature of the self, the sources of meaning and worth, the significance of the cosmos, the proper orientation toward mystery, loss, and finitude. But for some, that search leads out of one community of faith toward another. For others, the search for answers to ultimate questions does not end in a faith at all. It continues ceaselessly, perhaps sporadically. Or it comes to rest on answers that lie outside the faiths, between them. So, the affirmation of the value of freedom of religion or belief cannot be simply the affirmation of any one faith, or their totality. It must be the affirmation of the engagement with ultimate questions as such, and those powers of persons through which this engagement is possible at all. The European Court rightly wants to safeguard the religious liberty of believers. But on pain of discrimination, their liberty must be taken to be a genus of the species of the broader liberty to engage with ultimate questions, the liberty of conscience.[66] In their manifestation of conscience, the dissenting believer, the agnostic, and the atheist all may commit blasphemy. If Harry Taylor finds a god funny, his laughter can be a part of his manifestation of conscience, and it deserves protection as such, not only as an expression in public discourse.

Blasphemy must be legally protected as a matter of equal treatment before the law and as an exercise of the fundamental rights of freedom of expression and freedom of conscience. Neither a *sui generis* "right to respect," nor the religious liberty of believers, nor offence to believers, are sufficient grounds for limiting these fundamental rights. If the exercise of coercive force is to be legitimate, all citizens must have the opportunity to participate freely in public discourse, even when their contributions are blasphemous. On these matters, the case law of the European Court of Human Rights is conflicted. At one time it recognized that lawful speech may "offend, shock, or disturb."[67] Yet it has clung to an argument from offence in Otto-Preminger, Wingrove, I. A., and Murphy. It has postulated a *sui generis* right to respect for religious feelings while at the same time insisting that in a pluralistic democracy believers must tolerate and accept the disagreements and even hostilities of those outside the flock. The civil libertarian approach to blasphemy is consistent with the International Bill of Rights, and there is a good case to be made for adopting this approach in order to make coherent the decisions of the European Court of Human Rights.

It is a thornier matter whether the present understanding of international norms would permit peaceful religious "hate speech." While ICCPR Article 20 requires states to ban advocacy of religious hatred that constitutes incitement to discrimination, hostility, and violence, the Human Rights Committee and legal observers agree that this provision must be interpreted in such a way as to make it compatible with the guarantee of freedom of expression in Article 19, subject to the limitations laid out there. That is, the hate speech prohibited in 20(2) must be *an instance of* the kind of speech prohibited in 19(3)—speech that violates the rights or reputations of others or endangers national security, public order, public health, or morals.

The concept of "incitement" has been given no clear analysis in international law. Article 20(2) includes a criterion of intent, in its focus on "advocacy." In Jersild v. Denmark, the European Court considered the Danish government's conviction of a journalist in connection with a television program that broadcast racist statements. The Court found that Denmark had violated Jersild's freedom of expression because the racist remarks appeared in the context of a program intended to educate the public about social and political issues. There was no intent to foment racial hatred. And what must *result* from a statement in order for it to be considered incitement? In one case, restriction of free speech on grounds of incitement required an actual risk of harm or imminent danger for society.[68] Other human rights tribunals have employed inconsistent and far more expansive standards, according to which prohibited statements are "of a nature as to raise or strengthen" racial hatred, or such that one can "reasonably anticipate" a causal relationship between the statements and an environment of racial hatred.[69] The problem with these weaker tests is that, absent some showing of actual risk, they do not demonstrate that restrictions on speech are necessary to protect the rights of others or protect public order. So it seems that the understanding of incitement often exceeds that which would be permitted under Article 19(3). Properly understood, the international norm is consistent with a civil libertarian, content-neutral reading of "incitement" as intentional provocation of imminent lawless action.[70]

The *de jure* and *de facto* prohibitions on sacrilege in European states are historically continuous with longstanding traditions of honor-based civility, "law of insult," and public order. The prohibitions have been facilitated by the European Court of Human Rights' doctrine of the "margin of appreciation." The margin of appreciation doctrine, which has been deployed across a wide range of cases for over a generation, defers to the sovereignty of states by giving them an indeterminate degree of discretion to determine how much interference in a fundamental right is "necessary in a democratic society" to achieve certain interests. Some variation among states in their implementation of universal norms is inevitable—consider the international variation in the extent to which publishers and advertisers may, in their exercise of "speech," expose members of the public to sexually explicit material.[71] However, here a principled line can be drawn at restrictions on the "time, place, and manner" of expression. The margin of appreciation, by contrast, will allow states to cross over this line into content-based restrictions.

Although it is endemic to the case law of the Court, the margin of appreciation doctrine is inherently at odds with the universality of human rights norms, whereby minority perspectives are protected from public "consensus" as interpreted by judiciaries. Deferring to the margin of appreciation of national institutions "is inappropriate when conflicts between majorities and minorities are examined," as Eyal Benvenisti has argued. "In such conflicts, which typically result in restrictions exclusively or predominantly on the rights of the minorities, no deference to national institutions is called for; rather, the international human rights bodies serve an important role in correcting some of the systemic deficiencies of democracy."[72] Furthermore, the doctrine of a margin of appreciation can undermine the authority of international human rights organs themselves: "the rhetoric of supporting national margin of appreciation and the lack of corresponding emphasis on universal values and standards may lead national institutions to resist external review altogether, claiming that they are the better judges of their particular domestic constraints and hence the final arbiters of their appropriate margin."[73]

The European regimes of personal blasphemy are no longer defensible. Their laws are liable to manipulation and misuse. The legal instruments of offence and defamation send into the courts what is best left to conversation in the public sphere. And the pronouncements of UN and European human rights organs reverberate well beyond the region. The margin of appreciation doctrine dangerously plays into the hands of illiberal regimes that would use their discretion to suppress peaceful political dissent and religious minorities. Outside the European context, the penalization of blasphemy is not about token fines or canceled film screenings. Whether in Pakistan, where members of the persecuted minority Ahmadiyya Muslim community as well as Christians face death sentences for "defaming the Prophet," or in Iran, where members of the Baha'i community are imprisoned for "warring against God," the stakes of blasphemy could not be higher. A legal standard that is vulnerable to being exploited to violate human rights because of its structural features is not a good standard put to bad purposes. It is a bad standard. How tragically ironic it is that at the same historical moment when civil society actors in authoritarian states have thrown themselves into a mortal struggle to demolish blasphemy laws, the European human rights establishment would be upholding them.

States and supranational courts cannot be relied upon to lead the struggle for the right to blaspheme. It is being led by the civil society stakeholders whose freedoms are yet to be secured, those who name and shame state violators, who publicly critique unjust supranational decisions, lobby for the reform of domestic law, push electorally for responsible government representatives, and endeavor to educate the public. In doing so, they are demanding that states and supranational bodies bring their laws into accord with the moral commitment that justifies universal human rights standards—the commitment to treating all persons with equal concern and respect.

If it is possible to disentangle blasphemy from religious hatred, so much the better. But even where blasphemy is collapsed into religious hatred, blasphemy is not criminal because peaceful religious hatred, repugnant though it may be, is not criminal. State power is legitimate to the extent that it acknowledges the autonomy of citizens by approximating the condition of self-government. Not every action of the state can win the agreement of every citizen. The best the state can do is maximize the freedom of citizens to participate in the public deliberations that will influence its actions. That means refraining as much as possible from interfering in public discourse by way of content-based regulations that prevent certain viewpoints from being heard. Chasing after an amorphous "respect for religious feelings," European officials have trampled on the respect for autonomy that the state must show citizens as a matter of democratic legitimacy.

5 Idols

"Is it true that God is everywhere?" a little girl asked her mother; "I find that indecent!"—a hint for philosophers!

—*Nietzsche*

The Ka'bah was crowded. The six pillars of the holiest shrine in Mecca were overpopulated by images of the deities of pre-Islamic Arabic religion. The ruling Quraish tribe recognized *Allah*—a contraction of *al-ilah*, literally "the god"—the creator and sustainer of the world, but also a host of lesser divinities, trees, angels, and the "daughters of Allah," al-Lat, al-'Uzza and al-Manat. An eighth-century text, *The book of idols*, by Ibn al-Kalbi, describes a monument to the local god Hubal, a statue of red agate. It stood inside the Ka'bah behind seven arrows used for divination. One of the arrows was labeled "pure," and another labeled "associated alien." When the lineage of a newborn baby was in doubt, a sacrifice would be made to Hubal, the arrows would be shuffled and thrown. "If the arrows showed the word 'pure,' the child would be declared legitimate and the tribe would accept him. If, however, the arrows showed 'associated alien,' the child would be declared illegitimate and the tribe would reject him."[1]

According to the traditional narrative, prior to the coming of Islam, during the *Jahiliyah* or "Time of Ignorance," the peoples of the Arabian peninsula were mired in debased and ludicrous superstitions including Christianity, Judaism, and Zoroastrianism. As *The book of idols* tells it, travelers making camp for the night would select four stones. The best would become his god, and the other three would hold up his cooking pot. The goddess Manat was "a cubic rock beside which a certain Jew used to prepare his barley porridge."[2] According to Islamic tradition, the Prophet arrived triumphantly in 630 CE to cleanse the shrine of these false gods and to prepare the way for the One. Among the idols in Ka'bah was an image of 'Isa bin Maryam and his mother, or Jesus and Mary.

When on the day he conquered Mecca, the Apostle of God appeared before the Ka'bah, he found the idols arrayed around it. Thereupon he started to pierce their eyes with the point of his arrow, saying, "Truth is come and falsehood is vanished. Verily, falsehood is a thing that vanisheth [Quran 17:81]." He then ordered that they be knocked down, after which they were taken out and burned.[3]

Some say there were 360 idols. Some say 300. In one version of the story, Muhammad sent his cousin to fetch water from the well of Zamzam, and the pictures were rubbed off with a wet cloth. In another, Muhammad struck the idols with a stick. In yet another, he gestured at each idol with a stick, and as he did it toppled over. Upon seeing a portrait of Ibrahim, or Abraham, as an old man performing divination with arrows, Muhammad is said to have exclaimed, "May Allah obliterate these people. By Allah! They knew well that neither Ibrahim nor Isma'il ever divined with arrows" (The picture may have in fact represented Ibrahim subsumed as a manifestation of Hubal).[4] The remains of Hubal ended up serving as a doormat for the re-consecrated Ka'bah.

The trick with monotheisms is to pick the right One. If God is One and supreme, the danger of idolatry is ever-present, for many can be erected in the place of the One. Competition comes not just from neighboring gods, but even from our own ideas about the One. In those religious traditions anxious over spiritual fidelity, a receptivity to blasphemy can prevent straying. The history of Abrahamic religion reveals a series of blasphemies by one teacher or prophet against those who came before. The orthodoxy of today is the blasphemy of yesterday. While the orthodox will be content that their blasphemy vis-à-vis their predecessors was complete and never to be surpassed, they would be hard-pressed to show that they are impervious to the sin of idolatry. Therefore, they have an interest in at least listening to the blasphemer. Monotheist or not, everyone is vulnerable to the vice of investing the wrong things with sacredness, if by that is meant a special kind of vital, inviolable and incommensurable value. Sacrilege is the acid that eats away misplaced sacralization. By exposing ourselves to it, we stand to educate our practices and reorient ourselves toward what matters most. As I put it in a statement before the Human Rights Council in September 2008, to combat the defamation of religions is, in the end, to combat religion.

The liberal lexicon of individual rights and respect for persons has brought confusion to the moral treatment of sacrilege by conflating honor, appraisal, and civility with the form of mutual recognition that is a prerequisite for moral community. It has brought injustice to the legal treatment of sacrilege by rationalizing illegitimate restrictions on speech and conscience by appeal to a specious "respect" for religious feeling. Or so I have argued in the previous two chapters. The present chapter speculates that the success of the liberal lexicon could also mean the loss of other languages for sacrilege that we need to make moral sense of our world, and it proposes a model of ethical blasphemy as an alternative to personal blasphemy.

Idolatry and the likeness of God

Communion with the divine is always mediated by some representation of it. Such representations may be mimetic, metonymic, or linguistic. A mimetic representation connects to the divine through a relation of similarity, mirroring, or resemblance—a painting or statue of a divinity; a metonymic representation is a symbol associated with the divine—a token, avatar, relic, or place; a linguistic representation is part of a system of semantics in which certain symbols are used, according to convention, to refer to the divine—"Rock of Israel," "Son of Mary," "Most Gracious, Most Merciful."[5] As reverence and worship are directed through a representation, the representation can come to displace the godhead as the object of worship. For the theologians, this is a "substitutive error," wherein "the idol is regarded as a fetish that slowly and gradually acquires the traits of the thing it is representing. In a certain sense it becomes the body of the god, the residence of its soul, and an independent object of ritual worship. The purpose of prohibitions dictating proper methods of representation is to prevent errors of substitution of the representations for God."[6]

The passages of the Quran urging the unicity of the God, or *taw-hid*, may have been directed originally against the indigenous Arabic audience of supplicants of the daughters of God.[7] As Islam spread, this doctrine became important to distinguishing itself in the face of the Christian communities organized around belief in the Trinity. In Egypt under the Umayyads, for example, clashes over the identity of God took shape in confrontations over the meaning of public representations. There were widespread campaigns against the public display of the cross, which had become a near-universal symbol of Christianity in the Near East and Byzantium. Declarations were posted in churches reading, "Muhammad is the great Apostle of God, and Jesus also is the Apostle of God. But verily God is not begotten and does not beget." The symbolic supremacy of *tawhid* over Trinity was rendered in stone with the construction of the Dome of the Rock in Jerusalem in 691 CE. The Quranic inscriptions of its mosaic cut against religious competitors: "The People of the Book are warned not to stray from the tenets of their religion and it is stated that the Messiah, Jesus, son of Mary, was a Messenger of God; the Oneness of God is asserted and the Trinity is specifically denied."[8] The focus on doctrinal truth seems to have taken precedence over iconoclasm as such. Indeed, some say that at the shrine in Mecca, Muhammad placed his arms around one pillar in order that all but one idol be destroyed, sparing the picture of Mary and Jesus.[9]

We can ask why Mary and Jesus were spared. While Muhammad rejected the Trinitarian dogma that Jesus *is* God, he is said to have acknowledged Jesus as a great prophet in the line of Abraham, Moses, David. We can also ask why the other images were not spared. There is a paradox lurking in this and all spiritual iconoclasm. Why not just toss the idols onto the scrapheap? Why make it a point to put out their eyes and spit triumph in their faces? The benefits of clearing the way in the shrine for one's own rituals are obvious. Some political theatre may also have a social function of unifying or persuading audiences of adherents and potential recruits. Yet the ritualistic defacement of representations betrays a "fundamental ambiguity regarding the status of the image, which lies at the heart of much iconoclastic practice."[10] The iconoclast wants to show that the image is empty, hollow; that devotees have lavished their attention on a fake. Yet at the same time, by treating them as more than just material objects, he is in danger of attributing occult powers to them. Commenting on the desecration of images of the saints in the churches of Antioch, a late eleventh-century Christian wrote, "[o]n these the Turks had spent their rage *as if on living persons*; they had gouged out eyes, mutilated noses, and daubed the pictures with mud and filth."[11]

The paradox of iconoclasm is captured graphically in a story from the taking of Mecca. One of the Prophet's associates was dispatched to demolish the nearby sanctuary of al-'Uzza. From the ruins rose a naked woman with black skin and long, wild hair who came rushing. He struck her down saying, "denial is for you, not worship."[12] The goddess al-'Uzza, along with her two sisters, is the subject of the infamous Satanic Verses of the Quran. According to a story preserved by two early traditionalists, Tabari and Ibn Sa'd, Muhammad received a revelation of verses that seemed to affirm these daughters of Allah, only to retract them later after being informed by Gabriel that they had been delivered by Satan. The verses read "Have you considered al-Lat, al-'Uzza and al-Manat, the third, the other" (Quran 53:19–20), followed by, "These are the exalted cranes, whose intercession is to be hoped for." This later verse was supposedly replaced by "Why—for yourselves [you would choose only] male offspring, whereas to Him [you assign] female . . . " (53:21).[13] In the story of al-'Uzza's destruction, it seems that the idol was to be reviled not because it was hollow but because it was home to an indwelling spirit of wickedness. The denial of worship to al-'Uzza is at the same time a recognition of her palpable and threatening power.

The opposition to all figural representation is not based in the Quran but in the *sunna*, the purported sayings and deeds of the Prophet and his companions passed on by tradition. One rationale is a concern over usurping the creative power of God; the other, the fear of substitutive error. The antithesis of *tawhid*, and the most fundamental of sins, is *shirk*. Often translated as "idolatry" or "polytheism," this term is formed from a verb that pertains to "sharing" or "association."[14] It encompasses not just the worship of a god beside Allah, but the inappropriate association of anyone or anything with

God. The prohibition on figural images has been adhered to most faithfully in the case of the Prophet. Still, painted representations of Muhammad abound in the rich tradition of Persian, Mughal, and Ottoman miniatures.[15] In light of the paradox of iconoclasm, it is not obvious that the way to save oneself from the substitutive error is to remove paintings from one's sight. The temptation to *shirk* presents itself when the venerator develops too close an association between the image and the divine. A taboo on images can do just this, for it suggests that exposure to the image inevitably will have seductive power, and insists, against would-be desecrators, that what they do to the image they would do to its divine associate. In seeking protection from the image and in seeking protection for the image, the believer gives the image more power than it deserves. Thus, the taboo itself threatens to make a fetish of the appearance the Prophet, taking the rightful devotional place of his moral and religious example and message. An alternative strategy is to demystify the image itself, and to locate the sacred features elsewhere. The religious duty to avoid idolatry may be grounds for more pictures, not fewer. You can assuage a jealous beloved by promising to keep all rivals from your sight, but a deeper reassurance comes from the knowledge that the sight of them could not move you.[16]

An Ottoman writer recounts a story of iconoclasm at an auction of fine goods in Eastern Anatolia in 1655. Prospective buyers were permitted to keep items with them overnight while considering a purchase. According to the story, one man took for his perusal a lavishly illustrated copy of the *Shahnameh*, or Book of Kings, the Persian heroic epic.

When the witty fellow brought it to his tent and began leafing through, he saw that it contained miniatures. Painting being forbidden according to his belief, he took his Turkish knife and scraped the narcissus eyes of those depicted, as though he were poking out their eyes, and thus he poked holes in all the pages. Or else he drew lines over their throats, claiming that he had throttled them. Or he rubbed out the faces and garments of the pretty lads and girls with phlegm and saliva from his mouth. Thus in a single moment he spoiled with his spit a miniature that a master painter could not have completed in an entire month. . . . When the auctioneer opens the book and sees that all the miniatures are ruined, he cries, "People of Muhammed! See what this philistine has done to this [Shahnameh]."[17]

The clash between the attitudes of the defacer and the attitudes of the auctioneer (and the author) can be seen as a clash over what is sacred, and a disagreement among ordinary Muslims about the morality of Islamic iconoclasm. The defacer was deferring to the sanctity of the creator god, with whose creative activity we may not associate ourselves. His scandalized critics, revering the creative activity of the artist and his works, saw its defacement as the desecration.

Contemporary controversies, such as the controversy over Sooreh Hera's photographs of a gay Dutch couple wearing masks of Muhammad and Ali, must be seen in this context. Well-intentioned Western observers may think that by respectfully deferring to the strictest prohibitions, they are remaining strictly neutral on the culture of "the Other." They would be mistaken. They are in fact taking sides in important political-religious disputes within majority Muslim societies, coming down on the side of conservatives and Islamic governments against an array of spiritual counter-traditions.

In the hands of the rationalist theologians of the Mu'tazilite movement, the avoidance of *shirk* became a kind of Occam's Razor that could slice away claims of anthropomorphism and revelation.[18] The Mu'tazilite school, which flourished during the Abbasid Age (800–1050 CE), embraced a vision of persons as free and morally responsible, and a vision of a deity as beholden to standards of justice. Steeped in Greek philosophical learning, they asserted that the Quran was revealed for a particular historical context, and must be interpreted by independent, speculative reason. The *Kitab al-Usul al-khamsa*, or *Book of the Five Fundamentals*, by the leading eleventh century Mu'tazilite teacher 'Abd al-Jabbar, begins by asking what is the first duty to God. It answers, "Speculative reason, which leads to knowledge of God, because He is not known intuitively nor by the senses. Thus, He must be known by reflection and speculation."[19]

Tawhid entails that God, "being unique, has attributes that no crea-ture shares with him."[20] The language of the Quran that attributes human-like properties to God—"The Hand of God is above their hands" (48:10)—must be understood allegorically or figuratively. If God had a body, even an incorporeal body, He would be divisible and therefore not absolutely unitary and simple. The Mu'tazila were guarding, it could be said, against the substitutive error of idolatry, the sin of allowing a sign—even a linguistic sign—to misdirect one's attitude of worship away from the essence of the divine.

What of the properties essential to God—being powerful, know-ing, and willing?[21] The Mu'tazila reasoned that even these must not be metaphysically distinct from God. Universal terms like "knowl-edge" do not refer to a separate "mode" that inheres in the divine substance any more than "The Hand" means a hand. To their Sunni critics, this amounted to unbelief, a denial of God's attributes.[22] But they could also be accused of propping up an idol alongside God, and thus courting *shirk*. This can be seen in the controversy that agi-tated and divided generations of Islamic theologians and functioned as a battle line between orthodoxy and heterodoxy. The controversy sprung from a question that most people never ask themselves: How does God speak?

All were in agreement that the Quran is the speech of God. But *when* did He speak it? Did the Quran—literally "the Recitation"—have a beginning in time, a moment at which God created it by speaking it, or did it coexist with God, uncreated for all eternity? At stake were the doctrines of predestination and free will—if the Quran existed eternally, then it seemed that the content of the revelation would have been complete before the beginning of human history—and the doctrine of the absolute unity and simplicity of God. In 833 CE, the Calif al-Ma'mun wrote in denunciation of the "masses and the great multitude of the mean people and the lowest classes":

> They do not know God, they are blind for Him, and they err away from the essence of His religion, the acknowledgement of His unity, and the belief in Him. . . . They show this most clearly by putting God—the Blessed and

Exalted—on the same level with the Quran, which He has sent down; they are all agreed, unanimously and unequivocally, that the Quran is eternal, exists from the first beginning, and is not created nor produced nor originated by God.[23]

For their part, opponents could declare, "Whoso sayeth that the speech of God is created, he is an infidel regarding God . . ."[24] However, if the divine speech of the Quran is a sacred object, always existing, uncreated by God, with final authority for belief, it begins to sound dangerously like an idol. Instead, to put a modern gloss on Mu'tazilite doctrine, one could hold that the language of the book represents what God had to say to humanity at the time. Believers on both sides of this debate had intellectual and personal interests in the outcome. But they also could see themselves as acting under a religious duty to submit to the true god and to avoid spiritual promiscuity. In pursuing this duty, they were aided by a conversational space in which they could say things that incensed each other and courted "unbelief."[25]

These medieval disagreements over the speech of God are never far from the present. Some celebrate the eventual defeat of the Mu'tazilite side for ensuring that Muslims across cultures will be united in their veneration of Quranic Arabic, the *lingua sacra*.[26] According to what is now the traditional understanding, the eternal, "original" language, the sound of God's phonemes, has a special spiritual power that cannot survive translation. The devout of all languages are encouraged to learn *tajweed*, the art of pitched recitation or incantation of these sounds. The belief in the sacred aura of Quranic Arabic, however, comes with heavy encumbrances, both theoretical and moral. It stands in the way of understanding the book and its origins as human, historical phenomena open to investigation by reason and evidence, as the Egyptian scholar Nasr Abu Zayd contended.[27] And it makes for a troubled relationship between text and art, between *tajweed* and song.

In 1999, the acclaimed Lebanese singer and *oud* player Marcel Khalife was put on trial in Beirut for "insulting religious values" after releasing a song that contained a portion of a Quranic verse.[28] The lyric of "Oh My Father, I am Yusuf," based on a poem by the Palestinian poet Mahmoud Darwish, weaves a story of Yusuf (Joseph) into a comment on the mistreatment of Palestinian Arabs by other Arabs, using the Quranic words, "Father, I saw eleven stars, and the sun and the moon; I saw them bowing down before me."[29] Speaking before the court, Khalife, a Maronite Christian, asked, "Why do you persecute me?"[30]

> I shall not believe that quoting or incorporating a fragment of a Koranic verse in a poem, and reciting it with reverence and spiritual sensitivity, justifies this lawsuit. . . . Koranic citations and allusions have been a constant cultural and literary tradition that Arabs have kept alive from the time of the emigration to Yathrib to our time of emigration to the unknown in the twentieth century. . . . It is our hope that Lebanon will not succumb to insulting itself and insulting Arab culture by insulting the song 'Oh My Father, I am Yusuf.'[31]

At the time, the highest Sunni religious authority in Lebanon, Grand Mufti Sheikh Muhamed Rashid Qabanni, declared, "There is a limit to freedom of expression. One limit is that it should not infringe on people's religious beliefs."[32] He was missing something important. Elevating the Quranic language as art and culture, the poet and the singer were at the same time raising the possibility that conservative believers had made an idol of it as the eternal and uncreated word of God. More than just an "expression" about someone else's spiritual practice, their creative work also belonged to their own.

A normative theory of the sacred

While idolatry is a special preoccupation of the Abrahamic faiths, it has cousins outside of the monotheistic family, and even within secular ethical circles. It could be argued that traditional religious practices have taken a great measure of their strength from their co-option of a perennial human concern that is both more ancient and widespread than themselves: the sacred. If so, then conflicts over blasphemy within religions could be seen as a special case of a more general phenomenon of human negotiation and re-negotiation of claims about the sacred.

Even those who would prefer to see the notion of the sacred debunked will need to know what to debunk. If you and I disagree about whether something that happened was "good luck," we could be disagreeing over the criteria for what constitutes a lucky occurrence—must luck involve some grand design, or just happy happenstance?—or we could be disagreeing about whether this occurrence met those criteria and therefore constituted a proper instance of good luck—was it in fact only happenstance? In both cases, we would do well to aim at a shared conception of what constitutes good luck. In the latter case, a shared conception would make possible a constructive conversation about whether the particular case satisfied that conception. In the former case, a constructive conversation could not proceed without some rough mutuality on a conception, or at least a shared awareness of where our conceptions differ. This is true even if you deny that there is such a thing as good luck because you regard "a grand design" as hokum. In order to be convinced that the thing I care about is actually hokum, I will first have to share your view that the best or most relevant conception of good luck entails a grand design.

In attempting to characterize the sacred, two dangers loom. One is that the characterization will be overly narrow, and cater to one spiritual tradition over others—my god is sacred and the rest are false idols. In evaluating which things in the world, if any, are genuinely sacred and which are idols, we should be guided by a characterization of what would make anything sacred. And so, as much as possible, it should refrain from presupposing answers to substantive questions about whether any particular things are sacred, as opposed to valuable in some other way.

The opposing danger is that a theory of the sacred will be overly broad. In expanding the definition to general features found in a preponderance of cases, we might lose the very features that have persuaded people that the sacred is worth caring about in a distinctive way. If, according to our theory, it turns out that there is no difference between the sacred and just anything that is precious—precious in the way that the "ritual" of an afternoon tea may be "sacred" to some—then we will have failed to explain the distinctive importance that people have attached to the sacred. The notion—or a family of closely related notions—has played a particular role in human thought and practice, and we seek a characterization that best explains this role without prejudging in favor of any substantive view about which things are genuinely sacred.[33]

Although Durkheim made the sacred a defining feature of religion, a counter-tradition in the sociology of religion has found this definition to be too expansive.[34] If any social taboo can be regarded as sacred, and if the sacred and the religious are coextensive, then "religion" can be found just about everywhere. An alternative is to restrict the use of "religion" to practices framed within supernatural—though not necessarily theistic—worldviews, while loosening the cords between the sacred and the supernatural.[35] Various accounts of the sacred have spoken of a numinous or transcendent force, a *mysterium tremendum*;[36] a "great and portentous power" inspiring "fear and admiration";[37] a homology or synecdoche of the structures of the cosmos; the set-apart and forbidden;[38] a part of an inviolable normative order immanent in the world;[39] the fruit of valuable "investment" of time and creative energies;[40] and the dignity of the person.[41] In characterizing the sacred, the goal should be to arrive at a conception that applies to paradigmatic cases on which the considered judgments of competent observers would agree; that explains why people have cared about cases like these—their place in people's motivation and moral lives; that illuminates the disagreements among competent observers where they arise; and that does so in a way so as to increase understanding by bringing "sacredness" into greater unity with the rest of human knowledge.

Consider the following actions:

a. Defacing a national flag
b. Burning works of art by Picasso, Cézanne, Van Gogh, Matisse, and Gauguin

c. Felling a 1,500-year-old redwood tree to make lumber
d. Vandalizing a burial ground
e. Mutilating a human corpse
f. Making a lampshade of human skin
g. Depicting human beings as vermin or insects
h. Defacing a Star of David
i. Demolishing a sixth-century monument of the Buddha
j. Studying an 8,400-year-old skeleton considered an ancestor by indigenous peoples
k. Publicly slaughtering a cow
l. Destroying a consecrated communion wafer
m. Deriding a deity or Prophet in literature or art
n. Uttering the forbidden Name of God

What can be said about these cases? First, whatever is at stake, it is more than just a matter of fact; it is something reason-giving. It presents us with reasons, considerations that count in favor of or against actions and attitudes. It underwrites judgments of praise for responding properly and blame for failing to do so. In the above cases, a perpetrator acted contrary to powerful reasons and is therefore the appropriate object of a special kind of shock, horror, outrage and condemnation.

In some cases, the reason-giving force seems to reside in the object alone. In others, the object functions as a representation—whether by similarity, association, or linguistic signification—of something else in which reason-giving force also resides. Even where the properties of the object are not intrinsically reason-giving, they are intrinsically reason-giving when conceived *as representations of the sacred*.[42] The shapes and colors of a national flag are not intrinsically valuable as shapes and colors, but they are taken to be intrinsically valuable as symbols of the nation.

The reasons of the sacred, if they exist, are significant. They are not to be ignored. Their importance could be explicated by saying that they are more foundational or primary than everyday reasons. In the normative superstructure, sacred reason-givers form the base. Or, reasons of the sacred could be seen as nodes in a network, a web whose strands are lines of justification, warrant, and meaning. Borrowing some concepts from social network analysis, a sacred node would be highly *central*, where its centrality is measured by the *number of nodes* in the network to which it is connected, the extent to which it lies *between other nodes*, and the extent to which it lies *close to other nodes*.[43]

The impiety of roasting Helios' cattle can be seen as a failure to show proper recognition to the special reason-giving status of the sun god, in light of the meaning of the cattle's association with him. This was a failure in the normative domain. Helios, "who sees and hears everything" on his daily sojourns across the sky, acts as witness to mortals' fidelity to their oaths. Failure to take him seriously threatens to undermine an important ground for oath-keeping, and therefore displays a dangerous disregard for the indispensable social mortar of trust.[44] The offence by Odysseus' crew was an attack on something normatively foundational or central, something necessary to the integrity of the moral order. Had they prepared for themselves an ordinary supper of unsanctified beef, by contrast, the act would have been grounded by reasons of intrinsic pleasantness and perhaps continuity with valued cultural traditions. Yet those values could be excised from the normative network with relatively little loss of reasons to the surrounding justificatory web. Something sacred has great normative importance: it has a part in vindicating many of our ordinary reasons in a way that our ordinary reasons do not have a part in vindicating it.[45]

Moreover, the values of the sacred are *inviolable* in a special way. They are "set apart" and not to be sacrificed, traded, or compromised for other values. They elicit cognitive frames—perhaps belonging to our evolved psychology—of purity, pollution, and contamination.[46] The misuse of 1 percent of an agricultural plot impacts 1 percent of its economic value. Were the plot holy ground, however, the misuse of 1 percent would somehow be a diminishment of the whole. One explanation of why a sacred object presents itself as inviolable is that its value is *incommensurable* with others—it is not the case that they are of equal value and it is not the case that one is better than the other.[47] The nature of giving a gift to a friend dictates that one does not accept money in exchange for it. To even contemplate compensation would be to destroy the relations that make a giver a giver and a receiver a receiver. In the same way, the nature of the sacred dictates that one does not convert it to other currencies of value. To even contemplate conversion would be to commit a kind of *shirk*, an associational inter-mixing with the profane. To grasp the worth of the sacred is to render thoughts of trade-offs unthinkable.[48] Such "prohibitions against trading, mixing, and comparing allow people to set things apart as priceless, pure, and incomparable."[49]

From these notions sprout a host of theoretical thickets, which I am skirting by sticking with the generic label of "inviolable." Among many, there are questions of *categoricalness*. Would all agents, no matter what their interests, desires, or ends, have a duty to respect the sacred? There are questions of *defeasibility*: Can the duty to respect the sacred be defeated by other competing reasons? Could a sacred good ever be weighed against other goods that could come about through its violation? There are questions of *seriousness*: Are there in principle no degrees of seriousness of desecration? If slaughtering a sacred cow is serious, is depicting the slaughter of a sacred cow less serious? If the consumption of 50 sacred cows is abhorrent, is the consumption of 2 less abhorrent? Less abhorrent by a factor of 25? There are questions, too, of *agent-centeredness*: Is the duty to refrain from killing the cattle such that you may not violate it once, even if by doing so you could prevent others from violating it many more times? May you desecrate in order that fewer desecrations should take place? These are among many important questions about the concept of the sacred that would be obscured by thinking of sacrilege, along liberal political lines, solely as an abuse of a person's feelings or denigration of a person's standing in the moral community.

Given the hypothesis above, that sacred things are important, invio-lable, and incommensurable values, the modern liberal paradigm of the sacred—the dignity of the individual human person—emerges as a species of the genus. "There are many other remarkable things which you could say in praise of Socrates," Alcibiades declares in the summa-tion of his long speech in the Platonic dialogue *The Symposium*:

Some of these distinctive features could perhaps also be attributed to other people too. But what is most amazing about him is that he is like no other human being, either of the past or the present. If you wanted to say what Achilles was like, you could compare him with Brasidas or others, and in Pericles' case you could compare him with Nestor or Antenor. . . . But this person is so peculiar, and so is the way he talks, that however hard you look you'll never find anyone close to him either from the present or the past.[50]

This is a beautiful rebuttal to the Platonic picture of love, espoused by Socrates—who had lain cold all night beside Alcibiades' naked advances—in which true love must rise above the peculiarities of any one person's flesh and attach itself to more and more abstract universal ideals, until finally the lover no longer sees the beloved at all, nor any other beauty "in the form of a face or hands or any part of the body," but in beauty itself, in beauty's Form alone.[51] Contra Plato, the love of a person is not merely an attitude toward universal properties in which he participates. Love of a person is love for *this* person, for *this* particularity that cannot be replaced by or transferred to another.

Alcibiades' attitude is explored by John F. Crosby in an account of the concept of human dignity. He argues that the sources of dignity are dual: the reason or autonomy of persons, which we share with others in virtue of our common nature, and the *unrepeatability* or *incommunicability* of each individual person. Our autonomy, the capacity to author and to act on the basis of reasons, sets us apart from non-persons. Something else sets one person apart from all others. "Whoever gets acquainted with me in all my unrepeatable selfhood, gets acquainted with a dimension of my dignity that would otherwise escape him." Each person is, in addition to sharing in the autonomous nature of all persons, "unrepeatably himself or herself, and each has dignity just by being the unrepeatable one that he is." This is why "the news of just a single human person whose plane crashes, or who is killed by terrorists, can catch the attention of the whole world, why it can stun all who hear of it, and why we are not reconciled to the loss by the thought that the one who perished was after all just one six-billionth of the human race."[52]

As Crosby observes, uniqueness alone is not sufficient to explain the special worth of persons. There is, after all, only one even prime number.[53] But the uniqueness of the number 2 can be understood by grasping its place in a system of more general concepts. Any such explication of the worth of a person, it seems, would be incomplete. Any attempt at a full explication will of necessity be indexical, a gesturing to *this* person, *that way* he had about him, and the fact that he was this person and not that other. The substituting of others for him, therefore, is impossible in part because the things that make him worth caring about are ineffable and incommensurable. This ineffable *thisness*, which always outruns our efforts to conceptualize it, can go some way toward explaining the close connection between the sacred and the mysterious. If a thing is normatively central, then its ineffable specialness gives it incalculably greater importance, for it suggests that *nothing could take its place* as a central node in the nexus of reasons. This could not be more explicit than in a religious scheme in which the Absolute is taken to be the ultimate source of all goodness and all reasons. In a monotheistic scheme, the Absolute is also a person, and so partakes of the unrepeatability of all persons.

How does this hypothesis fare with respect to the cases above? Begin with what must be the clearest case, the horror of making a human being into a piece of furniture (f). The transformation of a person into an object is, in the purest form, the annihilation of the distinctive dignity of a person—the obliteration of the person's status both as an author of reasons and as an ineffably irreplaceable self. Normatively, a commitment to the worth of persons is central, even if on some religious schemes it is not ultimate. Would any of your reasons for action survive the loss of this commitment? The wrongness of depicting human beings as vermin or insects (g) can be understood in relation to the wrongness of (f), as a symbolic accomplishment of something like it. Similarly, the violation of a corpse (e) or burial ground (d) can be understood by way of their association with the deceased persons.

The destruction of masterpieces of art (b) and the killing of an ancient tree (c) could be said to annihilate something irreplaceable or incomparable. However, here there probably will be more disagreement over precisely what goods are at issue and just how normatively central they are, as clashes over environmental protection demonstrate. Claims of their sacredness will appear more or less sensible to the extent that one accepts the normative importance of these goods. Similarly, a competent observer could recognize that the defacing of a national symbol (a) is a violation of some value of a national identity, yet maintain that as a reason-giver, that identity is far less central than the Absolute, the trust-forging Helios, or the dignity of the person.

Some would say that the remaining cases, (h)–(n), stand apart from the foregoing because they are "religious," or—what for many is a necessary condition of being a religion—because they invoke something supernatural. However, to suppose they invoke the supernatural is not yet to settle the question of why people find the violation distinctively worth caring about. It could be that in the "supernatural" cases, the explanation of why the violation is worth caring about is the same as the explanation given in the other cases; namely, that it is a violation of some objective, central, and non-substitutable reason-giver. It is not obvious that the supernatural *qua* supernatural is worth caring about. If the purportedly supernatural phenomenon of divination or extra-sensory perception, for instance, turned out to be objectively real, I would like to know. But unless its objective reality were somehow connected to something of normative centrality, it would not occupy the domain of the sacred for me. The values that are challenged by an attack on a sign of ethnic-religious identity (h) can be understood apart from any supernatural implications that identity may have, as relatively more central instances of the kinds of values challenged by an attack on national identity. The value lost in the demolition of the Buddhas of Bamiyan (i) is akin to the incommensurable aesthetic beauty lost in (b), but also denigrated is the morally central example of the Buddha.

The objection by Native Americans to anthropologists' treatment of the bones of an "ancestor" as a scientific specimen rather than a sacred thing (j) can in principle be understood without recourse to a supernatural belief in immortal spirits. But even where the objection is grounded in a supernaturalist belief, the value being asserted is the value of a person—and perhaps, derivatively, the merits of a worldview that can spot ancestors at a remove of nine millennia. The assertion of this value is common to the "non-religious" cases (e) and (d). When a supernatural worldview is assumed, it opens up space for reasonable contestation even by people who might share a reverence for the values at issue. For by denying the worldview, they can sever the representational link to those values.

What of the objection by some Hindus to the slaughter of cows, especially when carried out ceremoniously or publicly (k)? Arguably, the veneration of cattle has less to do with the reverence for individual animals than with the symbolically associated unique divinities and the normatively central and violable principles they vouchsafe, such as the principles of love and maternal bounty, and their holy representative Krishna, a one-of-a-kind god if ever there was one.[54] Lord Krishna spends his youth stealing butter from the churn with his fingers and stealing moments of love from cowherd girls, the *gopis*. In the *Bhagavata Purana*, they express their devotion by anointing the child-god with the dust and waste of the animals. The infancy stories of Krishna the Butter Thief have been received by some devotees' meditations on love. "Krishna's thievery has nothing to do with thievery in the worldly sense. . . . His thievery is not mundane (*laukik*) because it does not transpire in an economy of scarcity. Rather, it is nourished in abundance." As his own mother points out, "with 10,000 cows of his own, Krishna hardly needs to steal anything from the *gopis*' store. If he does, one concludes, he does so gratuitously."[55] Like the cow herders, we can be tempted to treat love "as a commodity which can be quantified, separated into containers, stored, and treated as 'mine' or 'yours'—something that can be assigned a specific place and given a specific value." But this is a falsification of love—it cannot be purchased. If, in the gratuitous abundance of life, it graces us with its presence, we can do no better than to take it and lap it up with our fingers.

The Abrahamic monotheisms are most explicit in elevating the dignity of the person to a universal principle. As has already been suggested, by making the Absolute a person, monotheism unites in one agency the two interlocking features of the sacred: the central source of reasons is at the same time an ineffable, unrepeatable self— "Most holy He, *past all comparison*," in the words of a Jewish hymn.[56] The purported violations involved in mistreating the symbol or token of the Body of Christ (l) or insulting God, Prophet, or saint (m, n) are violations against persons. They are the spiritual homologues of mutilating a corpse and denying the humanity of a living human person.[57]

The Tetragrammaton might be taken for mysticism, and the Leviticus story discarded as barbarism. Yet offence against God can also be seen as the limit case of the most common moral task of all, giving appropriate acknowledgment to the standing of the other in relation to ourselves. Not addressing by Name is to El Shaddai what addressing by name is to you and me—a sign of due recognition of the authority of the one addressed. The sins of *nakob* and *takdhib* may be deficits of respect for the divine person, but their normative logic is derivative of a world of human persons, the world we create by according equal standing to each other and thereby calling each other into moral community. It could be argued that the offence of blasphemy makes sense, if it makes sense at all, only because we know what it is like to be treated with disrespect and we know that such treatment is wrong.

This normative conception of the sacred is non-supernatural, not in the sense that it precludes supernatural things from being sacred, but in that it locates the distinctive value of sacred things in features other than their supernatural features.[58] Some secular and liberal-minded readers may prefer to secure the moral permissibility of blasphemy by saying that there is no such thing as an affront to the sacred. But if something like the above account is correct, then the notion of an affront to the sacred is at least coherent. It is also morally relevant as it concerns our central reasons for action. Indeed, many secular persons already accept some things that satisfy the normative criteria for the sacred: the worth of persons, and arguably also beauty and truth. If there are other normatively important, inviolable, and incomparable values, a rational person would want to be able to discover them. So, we have good grounds for practising a stance of openness to the possibility of the sacred.[59]

The protagonist of J. M. Coetzee's *Elizabeth Costello* is a well-known Australian novelist who in the autumn of her career has become an ardent animal rights activist. She is invited to lecture on "The philosophers and the animals" at suburban Appleton College. In the course of the address, Costello likens the treatment of animals to the Final Solution:

> I was taken on a drive around Waltham this morning. It seems a pleasant enough town. I saw no horrors, no drug-testing laboratories, no factory farms, no abattoirs. Yet I am sure they are here. They must be. They simply do not advertise themselves. . . .
>
> Let me say it openly: we are surrounded by an enterprise of degradation, cruelty and killing which rivals anything that the Third Reich was capable of, indeed dwarfs it, in that ours is an enterprise without end, self-regenerating, bringing rabbits, rats, poultry, livestock ceaselessly into the world for the purpose of killing them.[60]

A resident poet at the college attends Costello's lecture, but in protest to what he hears, refuses to attend the dinner in her honor that follows. Instead, the next day he leaves her a handwritten note, which reads

> Dear Mrs Costello,
>
> Excuse me for not attending last night's dinner. I have read your books and know you are a serious person, so I do you the credit of taking what you said in your lecture seriously.
>
> At the kernel of your lecture, it seemed to me, was the question of breaking bread. If we refuse to break bread with executioners of Auschwitz, can we continue to break bread with the slaughterers of animals?
>
> You took over for your own purposes the familiar comparison between the murdered Jews of Europe and slaughtered cattle. The Jews died like cattle,

therefore cattle die like Jews, you say. That is a trick with words which I will not accept. You misunderstand the nature of likenesses; I would even say you misunderstand it wilfully, to the point of blasphemy. Man is made in the likeness of God but God does not have the likeness of man. If Jews were treated like cattle, it does not follow that cattle are treated like Jews. The inversion insults the memory of the dead. It also trades on the horrors of the camps in a cheap way.

Forgive me if I am forthright. You said you were old enough not to have time to waste on niceties, and I am an old man too.

Yours sincerely,

Abraham Stern[61]

So much is at stake in the exchange between Costello and Stern: not just the moral worth of animals, but the incommensurability of the Holocaust, our obligations to the dead, the likeness of God. The author makes plain that while Costello's moral witness is non-religious, it is consumed by a sense of sacredness and desecration: "We may not, all of us, believe in pollution," she says, "we may not believe in sin, but we do believe in their psychic correlates. We accept without question that the psyche (or soul) touched with guilty knowledge cannot be well." We are disturbed by "Germans of a certain generation because they are, in a sense, polluted; in the very signs of their normality (their healthy appetites, their hearty laughter) we see proof of how deeply seated pollution is in them."[62]

Rather than engage with what is at stake here, I will observe that we are in need of the right language with which to engage it. Costello's challenge is to the humanistic conceit that only the dignity of the person deserves reverence. While Stern refuses to break bread with Costello, and he alleges an insult to the memory of the murdered, he does not reduce her position to a personal affront. The language of personal blasphemy—of insult, honor, humiliation, recognition, and individual rights—will not suffice to carry forward a conversation such as theirs. What is needed is a far more nuanced account of the ethics of the sacred. Furthermore, the contest between Stern and Costello cannot be analyzed by placing the value of secularism and freedom on the one side and the value of religion and belief on the other. The contest is about whether certain things are sacred and what their sacredness demands of us. In this, the dyads built into the international legal discourse of personal blasphemy—religious and secular, belief and freedom—are of no use.

Readers who came to this chapter looking for a way out of the bitter public conflicts over blasphemy and "religious hatred" may be horrified to discover that far from offering solutions to these conflicts, it has only escalated them. What is desperately needed, these readers may be thinking, is to downgrade the hostilities from the transcendent, to move the armies from the valleys of darkness to the higher ground of secular moral rights and civic responsibilities. Instead, the proposals of this chapter would arm ever more sides with the batteries of "the sacred." If such proposals were implemented, the result would be more rather than less intractable enmity, acrimony, and grief.[63]

To these readers I confess that if there is a more ameliorative proposal to be had, I don't know what it is. If the analysis of ethical blasphemy that I have presented is in the neighborhood of the truth, then conflicts over the sacred are conflicts over central, inviolable, and incommensurable values. They are born of ancient human struggles to understand what we have reason to feel and do. Therefore, we should not expect these conflicts to go away quietly. Indeed, anyone announcing that he has found a way to resolve them easily by means of some master principle or argument should be regarded with suspicion. In our situation, a theoretical framework can be successful even if it does nothing more than to replace existing problems with new problems that are more intelligible. By shifting the debate out of a quagmire—in which people lob slogans of "respect" and "freedom" that fail to connect with each other—a promising framework might immediately produce more rather than less dispute, for it would transform what was inchoate opposition into pointed sparring over common subject matters.

The present framework, I hope, does this. It breaks up the inchoate opposition between respect and disrespect into a set of questions about recognition, evaluation, reverence, primary insult, and secondary insult. It supplants a sprawling antagonism between faith and freedom with an array of disagreements about particular moral values and the symbols that betoken them. It removes from the religiously aggrieved a conversation-stopping appeal to the pollution of sacred mysteries. Insofar as the religious are talking about something worth caring about it, it is something that others can understand and talk about as well.

The sacrament of laughter

Holiness asks for solemnity, William James surmised. Religion, he thought, "favours gravity, not pertness; it says 'hush' to all vain chatter and smart wit."[64] But if hostile to irony, he said, religion is equally hostile to grumbling and complaint. "If glad, it must not grin or snicker; if sad, it must not scream or curse. It is precisely as being *solemn* experiences that I wish to interest you in religious experiences." Still, levity has been put to holy purposes.

Paul wrote to the Corinthians that Christians were called to be "fools for Christ's sake," for "the word of the cross is folly to those who are perishing, but to us who are being saved it is the power of God."[65] St. Symeon would "throw walnuts at people in church, overthrow the stalls of street vendors, dance with prostitutes in the street, burst into women's bathhouses, and conspicuously eat on fast days."[66] Such holy folly, argues the sociologist of religion Peter Berger, "shatters the assumptions of ordinary, everyday experience" and prepares people for an encounter with the sacred erupting in the midst of the profane. In this the holy fool imitates Christ and participates in the mystery of a God "who descends from the infinite majesty of the divinity, not only to take on the form of a human being but of one despised, mocked, and finally killed under the most degrading circumstances." Paul wrote, "God chose what is foolish in the world to shame the wise, God chose what is weak in the world to shame the strong, God chose what is low and despised in the world, even things that are not, to bring to nothing things that are, so that no human being might boast in the presence of God."[67]

And what of the trickster gods? The Butter Thief's laughter is sacred; his is a higher mischief. Olympus echoes with the laughter of the Immortals. Sometimes, it is the laughter of cruelty or superiority, as with their hilarity at the predicament of the crippled Hephaistos, cuckolded by his wife Aphrodite. At other times, the gods do not laugh at but with frailty and humanity. The goddess Demeter, in mourning for her daughter, who had been abducted by Hades, could not eat or drink. Life on earth was withering away with her. Then, as Demeter sat unsmiling at a feast table in Eleusis, the servant girl Iambe "with many a joke moved the holy goddess to smile and laugh and keep a gracious heart." In some versions, it was a woman named Baubo who cracked Demeter's mood by playfully flashing her privates.[68] The irreverent and the indecent conspire to console a mother over the loss of her irreplaceable child. Even Jesus pranked his neighbors as a child in the apocryphal infancy Gospels.

It is no accident that laughter and blasphemy are so often found side by side. As blasphemy exerts a check on idolatry in monotheistic culture, irony and ridicule target moral idolatry in secular culture, the normative fetishism that invests reason-giving power in the wrong things. Satire can lick like flame at the edges of the sacred, eating away moral fetishes while leaving in sharper relief the borders we are not prepared to surrender. As humour incinerates the profane, it reveals what cannot be profaned. Risqué jokes circle around taboos, as the profanities of scatological humour prance inches from the entrance to the bodily *sanctum sanctorum* of sex. It is because the comical skates so close to the sacred that it is so often electric with danger. Not only insult comics leverage derisive laughter for social dominance. What makes slapstick funny makes dehumanization odious—seeing persons treated as objects. The absurdity and the spontaneous guffaws come from the sudden juxtaposition of a frame of reference appropriate to persons—the dignity of intentional agents in the space of reasons—and a frame of reference appropriate to objects—springs in the humiliating pinball machine of Newtonian dynamics.[69]

The offices of humour are not confined to the anarchic, subversive, and derisive. As every village has discovered, the long-term stability of the social order can be strengthened by providing the occasional carnivalesque release within ritualistic bounds. Under happy circumstances, such mischief can play the role of teasing of a kind familiar in any circle of friendship, collegiality, or family. In teasing, the parties tacitly understand that one party will prod the foibles and prick the pretence of the other without calling into question his basic equal standing in the circle, while the target of this treatment will endure it, perhaps responding in kind, but without taking it for an insult. Within these semi-formal social bounds, teasing can be a means of testing the terms of shared life, airing critiques and venting frustrations without provoking serious conflict. The atmosphere of humour and irony lowers the risk of bitter confrontations arising and lowers the social cost of those that do arise.[70]

This is the laughter of reconciliation and solidarity, the smiles that Apollo and Zeus, despite themselves, shower on a devious child Hermes. It was with a wink and a wry word that Hermes broke the countenance of Zeus and charmed his way into the company of the Immortals. The young Hermes had been brought before Zeus by Apollo and accused of stealing from Apollo's herd of sacred cattle of the sun. The offspring of one of Zeus' clandestine couplings with the nymph Maia, Hermes was born at dawn in her dusky cave in the mountains of Arcadia. Before noon he had wandered over the threshold and stumbled upon a waddling tortoise, which he throttled, then gouged to fashion the first lyre from its shell, promising the animal that dead, it would sing. But as Hermes sang on his instrument, he "dreamed of other deeds," and in "longing for flesh of kine" he set out to rustle Helios' herd. In darkness he separated out 50 heads of cattle and cleverly drove them backwards over their hoof-tracks while he disguised his own by wrapping his feet in the leafy branches of a myrtle tree.[71] In "a longing for the rite of the sacrifice of flesh" he killed, skinned, and ate two of the sacred cows, and then passed the night spreading the embers of the fire into smooth black dust.

Apollo soon found the herd gone missing and sought out the child who was back in his cavern dwelling, feigning sleep with the tortoise-lyre under his arm. Hermes replied to the elder's accusation with "twinkling eyes, and twisted brows, glancing hither and thither." Apollo could not help but smile at the child's cunning, dubbing him "captain of reivers," or cattle-raiders. He brought Hermes before Zeus to recount the story. The boy, still wrapped in swaddling clothes, had to explain himself to the lord of the thunder. As the Homeric Hymn to Hermes has it, Hermes pleaded that he had been coerced to confess: "he bade me declare the thing under duress, threatening oft to cast me into wide Tartarus." Furthermore, he pointed out that he hardly looked like someone capable of such a heist. "I was born but yesterday, as well himself doth know, and in naught am I like a stalwart lifter of kine. Believe, for thou givest thyself out to be my father, that may I never be well if I drove home the kine, nay, or crossed the threshold." At Hermes' wink, his father Zeus laughed aloud at the nerve and wit of this ingenious non-denial denial.

Later, when Apollo discovered that two of the herd had been eaten, Hermes had to soothe his anger. He took up his lyre "and wondrously it rang beneath his hand." Apollo "laughed and was glad," and as "the winsome note passed through to his very soul" he was moved to exclaim, "Thou crafty slayer of kine, thou comrade of the feast; thy song is worth the price of fifty oxen!" Hermes was elevated to a peer and colleague, entrusted to watch over all herds and flocks and "to establish the ways of barter among men on the fruitful earth." He was appointed herald of the gods and intermediary between mortal and immortal. In exchange, Hermes gave to Apollo his lyre. He swore off duplicity and thievery. The concord between Hermes and Apollo would be "a perfect token of a Covenant of all Gods and all men." The Hymn concludes, "With all mortals and immortals he consorts. Somewhat doth he bless, but ever through the dark night he beguiles the tribes of mortal men."

On the surface, the story of Hermes reports the frivolity of an insolent child who impiously flays the sacred flesh and gets away with it. Yet the Hymn suggests that he did not lack for seriousness of purpose, the seriousness of a child at play. After the theft, upon his return home to their cave, the prepubescent cattle raider is upbraided by his mother, who senses that the boy has been up to no good. He explains his intention to raise them both from the ignoble circumstances they have endured, and through the "wiliest craft" to see that they are fed forever. "Better it is eternally to be conversant with Immortals, richly, nobly, well seen in wealth of grain, than to be homekeepers in a darkling cave." He is, after all, a fosterling, a bastard, the unacknowledged son of the Father. "And for honour, I too will have my dues of sacrifice, even as Apollo." If the honor that is rightfully his will not be given to him, then he will steal it: "Even if my Father give it me not I will endeavour, for I am of avail, to be a captain of reivers."

With a winning word, Hermes finagles his rightful place as the son of his father and initiates a new form of intercourse between Olympus and earth. With a song, he brokers new boundaries for Helios' herd. Though he has disturbed their serenity, it was not done wantonly. Instead, he has taken Apollo by his ears and persuaded him that their worth is not incommensurable. The loss of some can be compensated by a gain in beauty. Fifty trade for a song. But neither do Hermes' actions defy the sun. They defy only the idea that a herd of animals can stand in for the meaning of the sun.

"And ever again," Nietzsche wrote, "the human race will from time to time decree: 'There is something one is absolutely forbidden henceforth to laugh at.'"[72] An absence of laughter resounds throughout the biblical account of blasphemy and the stony solemnities of the Covenant at Sinai. But the story of this trickster god reminds us of another moral orientation toward the sacred. It is the orientation of testing, within limits, the boundaries of the putatively sacred in order to test the legitimacy of authority and the justice of community. This higher mischief may go so far as to cause offence and strife, but it refuses to break the fundamental bonds of solidarity by denying equal moral standing to anyone. The desecrator recognizes the equal standing of others not by sparing them discomfort, but by holding them answerable for the commitments of their faith. Thus, responsible sacrilege subjects public claims to scrutiny in the space of reasons, exercising the key civic virtue of holding all authority to account by reason and so strengthening the covenant of a democratic society. Even more important, sacrilege can flow from an alternative understanding of what is and is not genuinely sacred.

Beginning from secular premises, we could be predisposed to con-clude that the charge of sacrilege is an atavistic horror that cannot be consigned to a museum fast enough. Or, we could despair of modern, personal blasphemy while welcoming the return of an older, wiser strain, a strain that turns away from the feelings of the subject and back outward to the normative order, to the question of what in this world gives us reasons. Rather than depriving the pious of a trope in which to protest desecration, we would see it extended beyond the bounds of the traditional religious communities in a final profana-tion of profanation. By making blasphemy a personal matter, modern liberal thought brought it from sin to secular crime. The task that remains is to complete this secularization, to re-imagine the sacred as a domain of the moral and to realize that we all have equal right and equal authority to speak on its behalf.

Postscript: On moral luck and cattle riots

How could literature, which bears close ties to life, avoid getting its shirtfront wet when life was drenched in blood?

—*Ismat Chughtai*

In September 1917, Muslim villages in the Shahabad and Gaya districts of the Indian state of Bihar were besieged by tens of thousands of rioting Hindus, who for days ranged in mobs looting and destroying homes, desecrating mosques, and stealing cattle. By their end, the Shahabad riots had resulted in "41 fatalities, 176 cases of serious personal injury, the looting and burning of over 150 villages and 150 square miles of Bihar passing temporarily out of British control."[1] After the military restored order, nearly 1,000 rioters were tried and convicted.[2] The cause? The ceremonial slaughter of sacred cows.

The ritual sacrifice of cattle for the festival of Id Al-Adha was common among the Muslim minority of northern India throughout the nineteenth and early twentieth century. In commemoration of the sacrificial acts of Abraham and Muhammad, every adult male of sufficient financial means was to make an offering of an animal. Alongside camel, buffalo, goat, and sheep, the cow was an attractively low-cost and popular option.[3] In South Asian spirituality, cow veneration and protection has deep historical and doctrinal roots. In addition to the stories of Lord Krishna, the epic *Mahabharata* tells of Nandini, a white "cow of bounty," a female "foremost of kine" who when addressed with "O, Give," always yields whatever is desired. Commentaries by Arab, Persian, and European travelers suggest that Hindu–Muslim conflicts over the treatment of cows date to the time of the Islamic conquest of the subcontinent in the seventh century.[4] British colonial records document eruptions of communal violence throughout the nineteenth century, with major campaigns against ritual slaughter organized by ostensibly peaceful "cow-protection societies" beginning in the 1880s.[5] Over a century later, the issue remained a source of intense political controversy, now fueled by the clashing political agendas of Hindu nationalist and Islamist movements.

As the history of communal violence in India underscores in blood and ash, the real consequences of sacrilege can be deadly. Government repression of religiously controversial speech is rationalized by the pressing need to tamp down inter-ethnic antagonisms and prevent provocation that could end in carnage. From the perspective of universal human rights, all governments should be moving in the direction of a legal regime of free speech in which regulation is "content-neutral," as a previous chapter argued. Their legitimacy depends on creating a public sphere that admits all contributions, barring incitement to imminent violence. Still, efforts by a state to move its legal regime in this direction can be held hostage by the culture and social practices of its publics. Where the danger of violent retaliation is real, and the ability of the state to enforce the rule of law is predictably weak, the would-be desecrator faces an excruciating moral dilemma. The people he may inflame are morally obligated to respect the lives and property of others, and so not to respond with violence. The state is obligated to protect citizens from such lawless behavior. Yet if he can reasonably foresee that these obligations will not be observed, and he proceeds with the offence anyway, we can ask whether he shares in any of the moral blame for what ensues.

Some might reply that the blasphemer bears no responsibility for the awful consequences that may follow since his actions were not their immediate cause. He is excused from responsibility for the harms—even the killing of innocents—because someone else's actions were their cause. According to this way of thinking, the consequences may be regrettable, but they should not affect our moral evaluation of the blasphemer. The moral evaluation of a person ends where *his actions* end. But of course it often makes perfect sense to blame someone who contributed to a harm without being its singular, immediate, or most proximate cause. Eurylochus contributed to the harming of his crewmates in that his actions were a part of the explanation of their deaths. In this sense, his actions were a cause of their deaths. Surely the crewmates were responsible for their decision to accept his proposal, but just as surely, Eurylochus was responsible for making the proposal in view of the consequences that he could or should have foreseen.

Others may assert that the blasphemer can be absolved just in case he did not *intend* the harm. Commonsense morality suggests that there is an important moral difference between intending an outcome and merely *foreseeing* that an outcome will result as a consequence of what one does intend. When we intend an outcome, we are committed to it in a way that we are not committed to a merely foreseen outcome: we use means–ends reasoning to determine how best to bring it about, we constrain further intentions so as to avoid conflicts with bringing it about, and we track our success at bringing it about, adapting as necessary.[6] A distinction between intending and foreseeing would lend support to the so-called Doctrine of Double Effect, according to which "it is sometimes less morally objectionable knowingly to bring about (or allow) some bad effect in the course of achieving some good end, than it would have been to bring about (or allow) that bad effect with the *intention* to do so in order that a good end is achieved."[7] The Doctrine seems to capture an important part of our moral practices. If you discover that I have killed your horse, it will probably make an enormous difference to your moral evaluation of me to discover that I did so with the intention of relieving its suffering. Relying on the Doctrine, it might be argued that the blasphemer escapes blame because he does not intend the harms that result, even when he knows that they will result. Had there been another less harmful means to achieve his ends, he would have taken it. But there was not. And that is no fault of his.

Many theorists reject double-effect thinking altogether, arguing that we are morally responsible for *what happens*, not merely what we intend.[8] If the blasphemer knows that someone will die as the result of his blasphemy, and he proceeds with it despite this, then he is as blameworthy as one who aims at the death. The bereaved relatives of those killed would hardly be satisfied if the blasphemer were to respond that while he foresaw that he would be a cause for their deaths, and he proceeded deliberately anyway, he did not intend to cause their deaths. The most that the Doctrine can show is that the blasphemer is not as blameworthy for the resulting harms as he would be if he intended them, not that he escapes all blame whatever. The act that leads to a murder might be less morally objectionable than a murder, but it might be morally objectionable and indefensible nonetheless.

Further, the Doctrine cannot plausibly be used to exculpate acts unless the intended good outweighs the foreseen bad. Arguably, this was the circumstance in which Eurylochus found himself. He and his men were almost certainly doomed in any event. Annihilation at the hands of the outraged gods was sure to come at some later point, but at least it would be quick and painless—with "one deep gulp of death"—and not inglorious. What Eurylochus intended was to ameliorate their suffering, even though he foresaw that his actions would also bring about their deaths. The badness of living until a little later and being grandly smitten then was not as great as the bad-ness of succumbing to a long, excruciating, and ignoble death now. If instead Eurylochus had chosen to infuriate Zeus just for a lark, in full knowledge of the catastrophe that would follow, then he could not be exonerated simply by observing that he did not intend it to follow. The lack of intention is not exculpatory unless there is also some good that countervails the foreseen bad. This means that some consideration of the consequences cannot be avoided.

The same problem can be cast in the terms of moral rights and duties. Someone might claim on behalf of the blasphemer that he is morally blameless so long as he does not act contrary to his duties to respect the rights of others. When innocents are killed following his blasphemy, their rights are violated, but they are not *violated by him*. Despite this, a sensible moral framework of rights must deal with risk. The blasphemer's action does not constitute a rights violation, nor is it intended to bring about a rights violation, but it does raise the probability that a rights violation will occur. And if it is wrong to do something that violates a person's rights, is it not also wrong to do something that raises the probability that a person's rights will be violated?[9] If I were only guilty of a rights violation when my actions *necessitated* or guaranteed the violation, then I could blamelessly poi-son you, serene in the knowledge that my compound is effective in only 99 percent of cases. If, on the other hand, we were guilty of a violation whenever our actions raised its probability above 0, then we could hardly lift a finger without being blameworthy since just about everything we do can present some risk of harm to others.

A rights-based moral theory might try to resolve this problem by distinguishing between different violations on the basis of their seriousness, holding that the more serious the violation, the lower the threshold of blameworthy risk-taking. Violating your right to bodily integrity, health, and life by giving you a cold is less serious than poisoning you, so perhaps while I cannot be forgiven for raising the probability of poisoning you to above 0.001 percent, I could be forgiven for raising the probability of giving you a cold to some point well above 10 percent. While this move is attractive, it is at the same time an admission that rights are not brute facts of moral analysis. For it suggests that rights are not all-or-nothing entitlements, but rather claims of varying strength that reflect some interests or values that are more basic than rights— being killed is worse than catching a cold because it is a more significant frustration of your interests or well-being. If such values or interests are acknowledged, then it seems that the moral evaluation of an action is not just a matter of checking to see whether it constituted a violation of another's rights. Rather, moral evaluation cannot avoid looking at the impact of the action on these values or interests. If so, then the blasphemer cannot escape evaluation for the effects of his action, despite the fact that they may be outside of his control.

This should not be confused with the claim that unforeseen and uncontrolled consequences can determine blameworthiness. That is a matter of controversy I cannot resolve here, the controversy over so-called *moral luck*.[10] Two drivers are approaching two different intersections. The first, in a momentary lapse of attention, ignores the traffic light and charges through an intersection. Too late, he sees a pedestrian who has begun to cross the street. He swerves, but strikes and kills her. The second driver, in just the same kind of momentary lapse, ignores the traffic light and charges through the intersection. But no pedestrian happens to be crossing at that moment. The second driver continues on his way and soon the event is remembered by no one. Meanwhile, the first driver is immediately subject to moral outrage, legal charges, probing investigation of negligence and contributing factors, and devastating public shaming. People in the situation of the second driver, it has been said, are *morally lucky*. Clearly, the second driver is lucky in that his life is not forever altered and disfigured by having been a part of a meaningless death; he will not be haunted by the thought, If only I had . . . But the question is whether he deserves any less blame than the morally unlucky driver. Moral luck has posed a puzzle to ethical theory because it elicits two contradictory judgments—the judgment that the negligence of the drivers is equally blameworthy and the judgment that the negligence of the unlucky driver is more blameworthy because of the horrible outcome.

It has been suggested that our tendency to absolve the morally lucky is without basis in reason, and is instead explained by three well-known psychological biases: optimistic bias, in which people unrealistically underestimate their risk of experiencing unlucky outcomes, relative to their peers; hindsight bias, wherein people "exaggerate, in hindsight, how likely they would have been to predict known outcomes before they occurred"; and the illusion of control, common on the casino floor, in which people insist that through skill or effort they can control chance outcomes that in fact they cannot possibly control.[11] These biases conspire to give people a tendency unreflectively to believe that when good moral luck blesses them, it must have been because of something that was under their control and hence, to their credit, and that when bad moral luck befalls others, this must have been due to some culpable failure of mastery or control on their part, and therefore, to their detriment. Once we recognize the effects of these biases, we will see that we are all as reprehensible as the unlucky driver, for we are no less guilty of negligence that risked the lives of others to precisely the same extent. Whether this is correct or not, most commentators agree that the paradox of moral luck must be resolved by narrowing the distance between our judgments of blame, either by attributing less to the unlucky or more to the lucky. No matter which way the paradox is resolved, we will have to reconsider rushing to judgment of the blasphemer whose act happens to result in harm. Depending on what he could predict and control, he may be no more negligent or callous than the lucky blasphemer who goes unnoticed.

Consequences matter to blameworthiness. But it is difficult to maintain that only consequences matter. The blasphemer who maliciously incites communal violence for its own sake does seem to deserve more blame than the blasphemer who is forced to make a mortal gamble on Thrinacia, or who verbally skewers another's idea of the sacred in an attempt at communication. We can ask, what are the attitudes of the desecrator implicated in his act of sacrilege, and for which he is answerable to others? Do they commit him to a value, principle, or judgment that is unacceptable to us? Imagine that I ceremonially slaughter a cow in accordance with my religious duty, thereby (predictably) sparking a deadly riot, whereas if I could have satisfied my religious duty by paying the moderately higher fee and sacrificing a goat instead. Assuming that I knew this, or should have known this, my action commits me to the apparently repugnant principle that some relatively modest sum of money is worthy of more consideration than the risk of harm. In blaming me, you are holding me answerable for this principle. My difficulty in justifying this sacrilege generalizes. Whatever the good that I hope to bring about, or duty that I intend to observe through my action, it must resist being outweighed or defeated by the force of the moral reason to avoid risk of harm to others. I will be compelled to ask, can I not attain this good, or observe this duty, through by some other, less risky means? And if not, should I not forego them or set them aside entirely? Is this act of blasphemy so important to me that I can permissibly risk the loss of life for it? Whatever the good or duty in question, I will find it difficult to overcome the strength of the reason to prevent harm to innocents.

The Muslim-born painter F. M. Husain was hounded out of his native India by over a decade of harassment and lawsuit by Hindu conservatives outraged by his nude portraits of Hindu goddesses. Husain's blasphemy—from their perspective—was a first-order blasphemy. "I have not intended to denigrate or hurt the beliefs of anyone through my art," he commented in 2010, upon renouncing his Indian citizenship at the age of 96. "I only give expression to the instincts from my soul." If Husain's self-descriptions are at all accurate, then his offensive work was undertaken because of some intrinsic interest it held for him, such as an aesthetic exploration of the celebrated eroticism of Hindu temple art. This was a *first-order sacrilege*, one undertaken for some reason intrinsic to its subject matter. In 2006, the organizers of the first major solo exhibition of Husain's work in the U.K., at the Asia House cultural center in Marleybone, were threatened with violence. A vandal sprayed paint on one of the works. Within days of being opened by the Indian High Commissioner, the show was closed.[12]

Against a pre-existing backdrop of threats and violent retaliation against Husain's first-order blasphemy, an exhibition of his work could constitute a *second-order sacrilege*, one undertaken in order to achieve some goal with respect to first-order sacrilege. It may be believed that the promulgation of the blasphemous material will make it easier to air similar material publicly in the future, that the artist's perse-cution itself deserves greater attention, or that cultural institutions must stand up to intimidation that would limit creative expression and impoverish culture. As a Delhi High Court warned in 2008, "In India, a new puritanism is being carried out in the name of cultural purity, and a host of ignorant people are vandalising art and push-ing us towards the pre-Renaissance era."[13] The reasons to engage in second-order sacrilege are not the same as the reasons to engage in first-order sacrilege. Indeed, even those who have no reason to engage in first-order shock to religious sensibilities may find themselves with a second-order reason to do so. The most powerful and general of the reasons to engage in second-order sacrilege is the importance of dis-couraging the resort to violence in public life.

Force should be a last resort. In any relatively just and well-ordered society, the legitimate use of force and violence ultimately derives from the authority of a legitimate sovereign state. Outside of the con-ditions of combat in war, individuals may not take it upon themselves to use violence or threaten the use of violence except in self-defence. We can understand the practice of violent retaliation against sacri-lege as analogous to the violence employed by terrorists in pursuit of a political goal, or by kidnappers and extortionists in the pursuit of personal gain. Once it is publicly known that some are prepared to use violence to avenge or prevent a sacrilege, then the would-be desecrator faces an explicit or implicit threat akin to threats of violence made by hostage-takers or terrorists to enforce their demands. Just as governments have a strong reason to resist such demands, desecrators have a strong reason to resist such demands.

Governments and law enforcement officials almost universally adopt a public posture of not negotiating with terrorists and hostage-takers for the straightforward reason that they do not want threats of illegitimate violence to be effective. To preserve a public order in which citizens are as free as possible from arbitrary force, governments go to great lengths to avoid incentivizing the resort to force. To this end, they attempt to ensure that force is generally perceived to be an ineffective means of achieving political and personal goals, and so not a rational strategy. The best way to ensure that force is generally perceived to be ineffective is to make it ineffective. So, governments have a rationale for refusing to comply with the demands of those who threaten violence, and for maintaining the public impression that they are non-compliant. Professional hostage negotiators will engage in conversation with hostage-takers, but the official policy at least is that they will stop short of complying with the hostage-takers' demands in response to their threats. The point of such "negotiating against kidnappers" is to secure the release of the hostages while at the same time "undermining the business model" of kidnapping for ransom.[14] To protect their citizens from arbitrary force, and to maintain a stable rule of law in the long term, governments adopt a No Compliance Principle.

When individual citizens and private institutions are faced with the possibility of violent retribution for sacrilege, a similar grim analysis applies. Insofar as we have reason to prevent unnecessary harm to others, we too should adopt a No Compliance Principle. By adopting a presumption of refusing to comply, and being seen to refuse to comply, we are doing what we can to uphold the rule of law and to contribute to a culture of open public discourse, in which no lawful expressive acts are prevented by threats of violence.[15] Academic institutions and media organizations in particular bear additional obligations as tradition conduits of public trust, truth-seeking, and communication.

This is not to say that everyone should maximize their first-order blaspheming. Alongside the No Compliance Principle is a competing consequentialist calculus: will the second-order blasphemy also *incentivize* future strategic threats by increasing their public notoriety—thereby supplying the life-blood of extremists?[16] A first-order blasphemy, like just about anything humans do, might be vicious, pointless, or banal. Imagine that a band of militant egalitarians is threatening to take an innocent person's life each time a new neo-Nazi website is launched. My guess is that liberals would not rush to reprint *Der Stürmer* caricatures, spreading second-order hate speech in solidarity with the neo-Nazis and in defence of the open society. If second-order blasphemy is thought to be more defensible, this must be because the first-order blasphemy is thought to be at least morally permissible, and perhaps even laudable when seen as part of a tradition of anti-authoritarianism.

Apart from the immorality of incentivizing violence, complying with the threats of the religiously aggrieved will often be impossible. The threat against F. M. Husain was at the same time a general threat against anyone anywhere who would depict Hindu divinities in the objectionable manner. How could such a demand be complied with? How could we ensure that such depiction never happens? This could be done by law or by culture. We could contribute to transforming the culture so that no one has an interest in the first-order blasphemy. However, such a process of cultural change is uncertain and lengthy, measured in lifetimes and generations, not weeks or months. In a society of millions, and in an interconnected global village, it is not within the power of any one of us to ensure that others will not commit the first-order blasphemy. So, while I might comply with the demand, others will violate it, and my compliance will have failed to avoid the awful outcome.[17] The alternative is to turn to the instruments of law to impose stiff penalties on those who engage in the first-order blasphemy. But such legal instruments would be illegitimate and in many cases would require a radical restructuring of not only my own society but many others as well.

The importance of second-order blasphemy can escape us because we fall prey to mistake of moral accounting. Suppose you are considering a second-order sacrilege, one intended to bring about some social good, say, a society in which people can engage in lawful expression on religiously sensitive subjects free from threats of violence. Suppose further that you have a high degree of confidence that your act will result in harm to someone. The problem is that you are not faced with a simple choice between the realization of the social good on the one hand, and the probable occurrence of harm on the other. You are just one actor among many whose actions are causally necessary to bringing about the good. By acting, you would not single-handedly bring about the social good. And by omitting to act, you would not prevent the good from being brought about. Now, it seems that the choice you face is not between the realization of the good and the occurrence of the harm, but between the occurrence of the harm and a contribution to the good which is imperceptible or negligible. The good society you wish for is not at stake in *your decision*. It doesn't matter what you do. The only rationally and morally defensible thing to do, then, would seem to be to refrain and eliminate the chance of the harm. However, everyone else in your society confronts the same choice situation. Identical reasoning applies to them. So for each person, the only apparently defensible course of action will be to refrain from second-order sacrilege. Every instance of second-order sacrilege, considered in isolation, is unwise. Yet if everyone fails to act so as to bring about the social good, the social good will not be brought about. So, if everyone does what is wise, then they will find themselves in society in which lawful expression is prevented by the threat of violence.

This reasoning is guilty of Parfit's Second Mistake in Moral Mathematics, the mistake of ignoring imperceptibly small contributions to a bad result.[18] If each of us pollutes a lake to some imperceptibly small extent, the lake will be despoiled. No one of us will have despoiled it, but collectively we will have despoiled it. The individual act does not produce the harm, but it is one of a set of acts that together produce the harm. Yet it would be a mistake to say that none of us has done anything wrong. In such cases, you must not ask whether your act will do harm, but whether your act will be one of a set of acts that will together do harm.[19] Collective action is required to achieve the good of an open society in which lawful behavior is not suppressed by the threat of violence. In considering whether an act of second-order blasphemy is morally defensible, we cannot simply ask what is at stake for that act; we must ask what is at stake for the set of acts of which it is a part.

The desecrators, like all moral agents, are answerable to others for their reason-responsive attitudes. They are answerable for the values, principles, and judgments that make sense of their dispositions, habits, omissions, and actions. When extremists are poised to respond to a lawful sacrilege with violence against innocents, there may be no satisfying resolution within reach. The desecrators are forced into a choice between the unfortunate and the tragic. Compared to the risks of harm, their reason to engage in first-order sacrilege may pale. And yet, complying with the threat of violence will often be neither feasible nor morally defensible. They find themselves on Thrinacia with every course of action unpalatable.

Notes

Chapter 1

1 From the website of the Organisation of Islamic Cooperation (formerly known as the Organisation of the Islamic Conference).

2 United Nations, "Human Rights Council resolution combating defamation of religions."

3 Stewart, "Blasphemy," 235.

4 Danchin, "Defaming Muhammad," 14, n40.

5 Rosen, *Varieties of Muslim experience*, 112–15.

6 An-Na'im, *Islam and the secular state*, 121; Reuven, *Islam in the world*, 125–6; Schacht, *Introduction to Islamic law*, 130–3.

7 United Nations, "Combating defamation of religions."

8 Rennie, "Newspapers challenge Muslims." On the cartoon controversy, see Klausen, *The cartoons that shook the world*.

9 United Nations, Malcolm Ross v. Canada, para. 11.5.

10 United Nations, "Report of the Ad Hoc Committee," para. 38.

11 Under "Offences related to religion," the Pakistan Penal Code includes "Deliberate and malicious acts intended to outrage religious feelings of any class by insulting its religion or religious beliefs" (Section 295-A). In its section on blasphemy laws, the Code states: "Whoever by words, either spoken or written or by visible representation, or by any imputation, innuendo, or insinuation, directly or indirectly, defiles the sacred name of the Holy Prophet Mohammed (peace be upon him) shall be punished with death" (Section 295-C); and "Whoever, with the deliberate intention of wounding the religious feelings of any person utters any word or makes any sound in the hearing of that person or makes any gesture in the sight of that person or places any object in the sight of that person, shall be punished with imprisonment of either description for a term which may extend to one year, or with fine, or with both" (Section 298). The section on "Misuse of epithets, description and titles, etc., reserved for certain holy personages or places"

specifically regulates the use of religious terminology by Ahmadis, who are officially considered non-Muslims under the law: "Any person of the Qadiani group or Lahori group (who call themselves 'Ahmadis' or by any other name) who by words, either spoken or written, or by visible representation, refers to the mode or form of call to prayers followed by his faith as 'Azan' or recites Azan as used by the Muslims, shall be punished with imprisonment or either description for a term which may extend to three years and shall also be liable to fine" (Section 298-B).

12 Asian Human Rights Commission, "Four children and one man have been arbitrarily arrested."

13 Associated Press, "Christian's death in jail."

14 International Humanist and Ethical Union and the Association of World Citizens, "The Cairo Declaration," para. 5.

15 Mayer, *Islam and human rights*, 8.

16 Reprinted in Chase and Hamzawy, *Human rights in the Arab world*, 216, 217.

17 For example, in late 2006, the Cairo Institute sponsored a dialogue between Arab and Danish journalists on freedom of expression and the press in the context of the cartoon controversy. A summary of the proceedings was published in El-din Hassan, *Religions and freedom of expression*. It speaks of opportunities for convergence among the interests of journalists and intellectuals from the North and South of the Mediterranean, but also speaks of frustration over European "double standards."

18 "Everywhere the foundation of the West is under attack. All over Europe the elites are acting as the protector of an ideology that has been bent on destroying us for fourteen centuries." From the opening of a statement delivered in court by Geert Wilders on 7 February 2011 during his trial for inciting religious hatred, see Wilders, "Statement in court."

19 See, for example, Fourest, *La dernière utopie*.

20 The influential distinction between recognition and appraisal respect is due to Darwall, "Two Kinds of Respect." My construal of recognition respect is influenced by Darwall, *The second-person standpoint*. S. D. Hudson uses "evaluative" for something like appraisal respect.

See *Human character and morality*. Respect as reverence is discussed by Feinberg, "The nature and value of rights." On honor, see Stewart, *Honor*; Margalit, *The decent society*; and Bagby, *Thomas Hobbes*.

21 Darwall, *The second-person standpoint*, 123.

22 Darwall, ibid., 132.

23 See Stout, *Ethics after Babel*.

Chapter 2

1 Leviticus 24:13–16.

2 Levy, *Blasphemy*, 11.

3 Lawton, *Blasphemy*, 14.

4 Robinson, *Essential Judaism*, 8–9. For discussion, see Byrne, *The names of God*.

5 Both in its broad narrative arc, and in its analyses of the significance of various specific cases, I follow David Nash's *Blasphemy in the Christian world*.

6 Nash argues that the survival of blasphemy laws is best explained by widespread acceptance of a providential worldview. See "To prostitute morality."

7 "If murder and blasphemy are compared in respect of the objects sinned against, clearly blasphemy, as being an offence directly against God, outweighs murder, which is an offence against our neighbour. But if they are compared in respect of the harm done, then murder has the preponderance: for murder hurts our neighbour more than blasphemy hurts God. But because our estimation of the gravity of a fault must go more by the intention of a perverse will than by the effect wrought, seeing that the blasphemer intends to wound the honor of God, he sins, absolutely speaking, more grievously than the murderer." Aquinas, *Aquinas Ethicus*, Question XIII, Article III, §1.

8 Nash, *Blasphemy in the Christian world*, 154–5.

9 Ibid., 153.

10 Ibid., 57; 109–13.

11 My discussion of the Aikenhead affair is based on Graham, *The blasphemies of Thomas Aikenhead*.

12 Aikenhead was not only a stranger vis-à-vis Presbyterian Christianity; he was said to have praised the Islamic faith and professed more admiration for Muhammad than for Jesus. See Graham, ibid., 81.

13 See Swanson, "Literacy, heresy, history and orthodoxy," 279.

14 See Robert Chazan, *The Jews of medieval Western Christendom*.

15 Marcus, *The Jew in the medieval world*, 139.

16 Moore, *The birth of popular heresy*, 2.

17 Accused heretics at Orléans are alleged to have said, in what became the first recorded case of burning for heresy in medieval Europe, when asked whether they believed that God made everything from nothing:

> We believe in the law written within us by the Holy Spirit, and hold everything else, except what we have learnt from God, the maker of all things, empty, unnecessary, and remote from divinity. Therefore bring an end to your speeches and do with us what you will. Now we see our king reigning in heaven. He will raise us to his right hand in triumph and give us eternal joy.

Peters, *Heresy and authority*, 71.

18 Nash, *Blasphemy in the Christian world*, 150–1.

19 Geary, *Readings in medieval history*, 483.

20 Ibid., 484.

21 Ibid., 499.

22 Blumenthal, *The investiture controversy*.

23 Pennington, "Law, legislative authority," 426.

24 In Robinson, *Readings in European history*, 72–3.

25 The author was Alcuin of York. See Robinson, "Church and papacy," 289.

26 See Berman, *Law and revolution*.

27 1 Peter 2:16.

28 Nash, *Blasphemy in the Christian world*, 46.

29 Ibid., 47.

30 Attributed to Petrus Cantor, Precenter of Notre Dame. See Montagu, *The history of swearing*, 109.

31 The Hale judgment is discussed in Nash, *Blasphemy in the Christian world*, 160–2.

32 Radan, Meyerson, and Crocher, *Law and religion*, 185.

33 Ibid.

34 Masefield, "Crops and livestock."

35 Lewis, *Islam and the West*, 23.

36 Williams, *The bloudy tenent of persecution*, 83–4.

37 One way we could help ourselves to this assumption is if *anything* that God wills to happen were justified for the reason that there is nothing more to being justified than being willed by God. But this line of thinking runs into a problem, as philosophers since Plato have never tired of pointing out. If God is to be a person, an agent, and not simply an impersonal force or happening, then he must be capable of deliberating and deciding on the basis of reasons. Deciding on the basis of reasons involves figuring out what is the right thing to do—recognizing some considerations independent of our will that count in favor of an option, relative to other options, and being caused by that recognition to intend to take that option. If any option that God intends is the right thing to do, then it seems that his intentions could not be guided by the recognition of independent considerations that count in favor of one option over others. God declared Creation good for no reason. He could have declared it worthless, for no reason at all, and it would have been so. At best, this would make rightness arbitrary; at worst, it would make God incapable of genuine deliberation and decision at all.

Some have responded that rightness is not arbitrary since it is in accord with God's nature, and his nature is essentially and necessarily good. One difficulty with this response is that when people assert that God is good, or just, or worthy of worship, it seems that they must be asserting more than just that God does what God wills. These assertions make sense in the context of evaluative standards—apart from God's will—that would warrant the ascription of justice, goodness, or worship-worthiness to anyone. Saying that God is worthy of praise is saying more than that God is God. *Halleluiah* had better not be tautology.

38   Grotius, *The rights of war and peace*, 170–1.

39   Ibid., 1747.

40   Ibid., 1748.

41   Ibid., 138.

42   Ibid., 155–6.

43   Romans 2:14–15.

44   Tierney, *The idea of natural rights*, 64.

45   Read from this perspective, the Mosaic story of the origins of positive law presupposes the natural law. For if the Covenant at Sinai is to be a just agreement between God and the Israelites, it must be consistent with their pre-existing natural rights. And if the agreement is to be normatively binding on them, they must be under a prior obligation to keep their covenants. These rights and obligations, therefore, cannot simply be created by divine decree.

46   Nash, *Blasphemy in the Christian world*, 58.

47   Ibid., 157. Of course, whether a blasphemy provokes the public depends in the first instance on the temperament of the public. There were times and places in the history of European life where such disturbances were a real danger, particularly when the belief in providential intervention to punish blasphemy was widespread among ordinary people, and so civil authorities could have a reasonable purpose in suppressing it. By the same token, the more remote the possibility of actual furore, the less compelling the empirical case for suppression of blasphemy on grounds of public order. And so, the central prop of the public order rationale—a causal link between sacrilegious speech and civil disorder—is subject to being toppled by shifting sociological realities.

48   Discussed in Post, *Constitutional domains*, 95.

49   Marsh, *Word crimes*, 160.

50   Regina v. Bradlaugh, discussed in Post, *Constitutional domains*, 96.

51   In David Nash's terms, blasphemy had been transformed from "passive" to "active." The new model of active blasphemy did not necessarily provide for the rights of free expression, yet it placed much

more responsibility upon those who claimed they were offended by the actions and words of others. As providential belief declined in everyday life, believers had to express their horror as a manifestation of profound personal offence (*Blasphemy in the Christian world*, 81–2).

52 Hashemi, *Religious legal traditions*, 86.
53 Stewart, *Honor*, chapter 4.
54 Bagby, *Thomas Hobbes*.
55 Whitman, "Enforcing civility and respect," 1279.
56 Stewart, 63.
57 Tierney, *The idea of natural rights*, 65.
58 This intellectual tradition can be seen as a member of family of notions that Charles Taylor has called "inwardness," and has traced back through Descartes, St. Augustine, and Plato. See Taylor, *Sources of the self*. In *A secular age*, Taylor introduced the notion of "the buffered self" to explicate the modern conception of agency and responsibility.
59 On constructivism, objectivism, and subjectivism about reasons, see Korsgaard, *The constitution of agency* and Schafer-Landau, ed., *Oxford studies in metaethics*.

Chapter 3

1 Homer, *The Odyssey*, lines 12.137–51.
2 Ibid., 12.345–6.
3 Ibid., 12.366–78.
4 Ibid., 12.382–92.
5 Ibid., 10.480.
6 Neu, *Sticks and stones*, 34.
7 Stewart, *Honor*, 54.
8 United Nations, Report of the Special Rapporteur on violence against women, para. 18. See also Welchman and Hossain, *Honour*; Nye, *Masculinity and male codes of honor*.

9   I am prepared to admit that post-honor societies may have something to gain, or regain, by incorporating features of the honor-conscious. Courage and valour, de-gendered, may be virtues in need of reviving. Public shaming may have important advantages over incarceration and punitive fining. But such features would have to be adjuncts to a system based on equal recognition, not a replacement for it. The feat would be to extricate these redeemable shards from the structures of gender apartheid and warrior worship in which they were embedded. See, for instance, Bowman, *Honor*.

10 Ambedkar, "The annihilation of caste"; cited in Keane, *Caste-based discrimination*, 5.

11 Keane, *Caste-based discrimination*, 5.

12 Zelliot, "Religion and legitimation in the Mahar Movement," 94. Strictly speaking, Indian philosophy has no concept of blasphemy analogous to that found in Abrahamic faiths, but it distinguishes as *nastika* or heterodox those schools of thought—including Carvaka, Jainism, and Buddhism—that reject the supreme authority of the Vedas. One commentator suggests that in recent years, public complaints of religious defamation by members of the Muslim minority have led some politically-motivated Hindus to seek similar protection for Hindu deities. See Tripathi, "Meanwhile."

13 Charles Taylor calls this "recognition," whereas the nomenclature of respect I am using reserves this term for acknowledgment of equal normative authority. See Taylor, "The politics of recognition," 98.

14 Variations on this influential argument have been championed by Michael Sandel in *Liberalism and the limits of justice* and by Nicholas Wolterstorff in Robert Audi and Nicholas Wolterstorff, *Religion in the public square*. In her essay "The sublime and the good," Iris Murdoch observed, "Kant does not tell us to respect whole particular tangled-up historical individuals, but to respect the universal reason in their breasts. In so far as we are rational and moral we are all the same." See Antonaccio, *Picturing the human*, 104.

15 We are, on the other hand, committed to rejecting the substantive judgment that his identity has some *greater* worth that would give him superior standing.

16 Taylor, "The politics of recognition," 98.

17 Nagel, *Equality and partiality*, 11.

18 Ibid.

19 Darwall, *The second-person standpoint*, 127.

20 Wolf, "Fundamental rights," 117.

21 Sen, *Identity and violence.*

22 See, for example, L. Bennett Graham, "Defamation of religions"; European Commission for Democracy through Law, *Blasphemy, insult and hatred*, 26–7.

23 Strawson, "Freedom and Resentment," 379.

24 Ibid., 376.

25 Sher, *In praise of blame*, 12.

26 Smith, "Character, blameworthiness, and blame," 33.

27 Smith, "Responsibility for attitudes," 239–40. The discussion that follows is based on Smith's "rational relations" account of responsibility.

28 Ibid., 250–1.

29 In Singh, ed., *Ambedkar on religion*, 276. Ambedkar seems to have embraced a Durkheimian conception that makes the sacred necessarily connected to the religious and the inviolable: "Hindus are the only people in the world whose social order—the relation of man to man—is consecrated by religion and made sacred, eternal and inviolate" (261). However, for him religion required no revelation, salvation or personal deity. It was rather a humanist ethical system teaching altruism and justice. See Rodriques, "Dalit-Bahujan discourse," 69. Early in his public life, Ambedkar made clear his thoughts on the deity: "How many generations of ours have worn themselves out by rubbing their foreheads on the steps of the god? But when did the god take pity on you? What big thing has he done for you? . . . It is not this god that you worship, it is your ignorance" (Jaffrelot, *Dr. Ambedkar and untouchability*, 49). Ambedkar embraced Buddhism just months before his death in 1956.

30 In the preface to the 1937 edition of *The annihilation of caste*, the author does go so far as to call Hindus "the sick men of India." I do not mean to hold up Ambedkar as a model in all respects. He advocated extensive government control of Hindu practice—including

banning teaching of the Vedas and state examination and licensing of the priesthood—contrary to international human rights standards of freedom of association, assembly, expression and religion or belief. I cite his work only to illustrate my thesis that religiously controversial speech is often a contest of competing claims about sacred values.

31 Gora, *We become atheists*.

32 Meiklejohn, *Free speech and its relation to self-government*, 22.

33 Ibid., 23.

34 Gardels, "Cartoon controversy is not a matter of free speech, but civic responsibility."

35 Riedweg, *Pythagoras*, 69, 71. Aristotle also floats the suggestion that the Pythagorean injunction meant to abstain from politics, as dried beans were used in the casting of votes.

36 Ibid., 70.

37 Habermas, *Moral consciousness and communicative action*; *Between facts and norms*.

38 Pettit and Smith, "Freedom in belief and desire."

Chapter 4

1 This way of understanding human rights I take from Jack Donnelly, *Universal human rights in theory and practice*, and Michael Ignatieff, *Human rights as politics and idolatry*.

2 Before the plenary session of the General Assembly, representative Kahn argued that, contrary to the position of Saudi Arabia and several other Islamic states, the right was compatible with Islam since it was "a missionary religion: it strove to persuade men to change their faith and alter their way of living, so as to follow the faith and way of living it preached, but it recognized the same right of conversation for other religions as for itself." In Tahzib, *Freedom of religion or belief*, 74–5.

3 Otto-Preminger-Institut v Austria, para. 46, 47, 55.

4 Ibid., para. 56.

5 Ibid., para. 50, 56.

6 Mill, "On liberty," 70.

7 In his 1785 (1994) "Essay on the application of probability theory to plurality decision-making" (*Essai sur l'application de l'analyse à la probabilité des décisions rendues à la pluralité des voix*).

8 Mill, "On liberty," 20.

9 This tradition is most closely associated with Ronald Dworkin and Robert Post. In what follows, I use Post's account as representative. See Post, *Constitutional domains*; Dworkin, *Sovereign virtue*; "Even Bigots and Holocaust Deniers Must Have Their Say."

10 Bobbio, *Democracy and dictatorship*, 137, cited in Post, *Constitutional domains*, 280.

11 For a deflation of the contemporary liberal picture of politics as a Habermasian seminar, see Brennan and Lomasky, *Democracy and decision*.

12 See Rousseau, *The social contract*, note 6.

13 Post, "Religion and freedom of speech," 75.

14 Post, "Racist speech, democracy, and the First Amendment," 290. The conclusion of the legitimacy argument can be cast in several ways, some more plausible than others. Citizens are not justified in ignoring the authority of a state whenever it suppresses one of their ideas in public discourse. However, suppression of an idea does *diminish* the legitimacy of the laws to which it is normatively relevant. This seems to be Dworkin's view. See Waldron, "Dignity and defamation," 1642–6.

15 Kant, "What is Enlightenment?" 57.

16 Rawls, *Political liberalism*, 11. The legitimacy of coercive power need not presuppose, as Rawls and many other liberals have maintained, that all of the reasons put forward in public discourse must be "public" in Rawls' special sense of appealing only to considerations that all citizens could accept: "since the exercise of political power itself must be legitimate, the ideal of citizenship imposes a moral, not a legal, duty . . . to be able to explain to one another on those fundamental questions how the principles and policies they advocate and vote for can be supported by the political values of public reason" (ibid., 217). A public reason is drawn from a "political conception of justice" on which there is an overlapping consensus of reasonable comprehensive doctrines. So, for a use of state power to be legitimate, it must be

supported by reasons that are endorsed by all: "if we argue that the religious liberty of some citizens is to be denied, we must give them reasons they can not only understand—as Servetus could understand why Calvin wanted to burn him at the stake—but reasons we might reasonably expect that they as free and equal might reasonably also accept" (ibid., 447). Of course, from the fact that a policy must be justifiable to all, it does not follow that there is one reason for the policy that justifies it to all. Different persons might embrace different reasons for the same policy. In that case, there is no objection from legitimacy.

17 See Siegel, *Communication law in America*.

18 Brandenburg v. Ohio.

19 I.A. v Turkey, para. 13.

20 Ibid., para. 22.

21 Ibid., para. 27.

22 Ibid., para. 29–30.

23 Ibid., para. 42.

24 Wingrove v. United Kingdom, para. 57.

25 Murphy v. Ireland, para. 12.

26 Weinstein, "Extreme speech, public order," 30–1. In the below, I follow Weinstein's analysis of the significance of the Hammond case.

27 Ibid., 32–3.

28 Ibid., 23.

29 Mill, "On liberty," 13–14.

30 Feinberg, *The moral limits of the criminal law*, 5–6.

31 Feinberg illustrates his typology of offences with a series of 31 vignettes set on a crowded city bus where seatmates are doing things that could make a Caligula queasy. The distinction between harm and offence is debatable. According to a perfectly ordinary sense of "harm," an extremely unpleasant experience would be a minor harm. Furthermore, as David Shoemaker observes, "it is unclear why the scales of offence and harm are incommensurable, that, as Feinberg puts it, '[Offences] are a different sort of thing altogether, with a scale all of their own,' given that extreme offences may also 'be actually harmful, in a minor sort of way.' Is it their

extreme nature that makes them harmful? If so, why not think of them as being on the lowest part of the harm scale and not on a different scale altogether?" (Shoemaker, "Dirty words and the Offence Principle," note 11).

32 Feinberg, *The moral limits of the criminal law*, 5.

33 Ibid., xiii.

34 Ibid., 26.

35 Shoemaker lodges this objection against Feinberg's analysis in "Dirty words and the Offence Principle." He maintains that offence to religious sensibilities in particular is never sufficient grounds for legal penalty. Reasonableness consists in advancing only reasons that are public in the Rawlsian sense of endorsed by all citizens, and religious commitments, because they are not universally endorsed, fail the test of publicity; therefore, offences to religious sensibilities can never be reasonable. However, this understanding of reasonableness is both unworkable and unjust, as I endeavor to show in *The secular conscience*.

36 Post, "Religion and freedom of speech," 76.

37 Choudhury v. United Kingdom.

38 Kokkinakis v. Greece, para. 31.

39 Otto-Preminger v Austria, para. 47.

40 Taylor, *Freedom of religion*, 94–6.

41 Turkey's 1926 Penal Code was adapted from the Italian Penal Code of 1889 (Gareth Jenkins, *Political Islam in Turkey*, 97). The reformed criminal code that went into effect on 1 April 2005 did not contain Article 175's anti-blasphemy provision. However, the new Article 125 on "Crimes against honour" contained the offence of religious insult and Article 216 of the Code provided that "those who incite a segment of people bearing different characteristics in terms of social class, race, religion, sect or region to hatred and hostility against another segment" shall be punished "provided that this causes a clear and present danger to public security." See European Commission for Democracy through Law, *Blasphemy, insult and hatred*, 305. In this case, the Turkish state adopted a more liberal approach than the Strasbourg court was prepared to require of it.

42 Interestingly, the Court has found elsewhere that the protection of manifestations of religion does extend to the attack on the principles of secularism. See Refah Partisi and Others v. Turkey. I thank Afshin Ellian for bringing this case to my attention.

43 See Whitman, "Enforcing civility and respect."

44 United Nations, "Report of the Special Rapporteur," para. 45, 65. During the sixteenth session of the Human Rights Council, the OIC appeared to abandon its 12-year-old tradition, agreeing to a new resolution with language negotiated by the US and Pakistani delegations. The resolution, which was adopted by consensus on 24 March 2011, makes no mention of "defamation" and calls for criminalization only of "incitement to imminent violence based on religion or belief" (United Nations, "Combating intolerance").

45 European Commission for Democracy through Law, *Blasphemy, insult and hatred*, 20, 19.

46 Here, for instance, is a defense by Baroness O'Cathain before the British Parliament: "The legal notion of blasphemy dates back many centuries, as has been pointed out. It is part of a Christian heritage that formed our constitution. . . . The Christian heritage of this country goes back much more than 1,000 years, and its legacy is still very much present in our national life." Quoted in Oliva, "The legal protection," 73.

47 Racial and Religious Hatred Act 2006, s 29J.

48 Public Order Act 1986, s 5.

49 Crime and Disorder Act 1998, s 28.

50 Dawar, "Teenager faces prosecution."

51 Taylor, "Atheist given Asbo."

52 Norwood v. United Kingdom.

53 Ibid. Hannes Cannie and Dirk Voorhoof argue that the Court's use of the abuse clause is problematic because it results in categorical exclusion from Article 10 protections instead of a consideration of freedom of expression in light of the entire case. See Cannie and Voorhoof, "The Abuse Clause."

54 BBC News World Edition, "French author denies racial hatred."

55 Mbongo, "Hate speech," 229.

56 Mbongo, "Hate speech," 231.

57 The version of the rights-based analysis of hate speech as group defamation I will present is an amalgam of the work of Steven J. Heyman, Catharine MacKinnon, and Jeremy Waldron.

58 Even defenders of criminalizing hate speech qua group defamation can be sanguine about distinguishing religious criticism and insult from group defamation in practice. Jeremy Waldron writes,

> The group of all Muslims in society, the group of all followers of Islam, is a group of people committed to the one God, to his Prophet, Mohammed, and to the holy writings of the Koran. On the account that I am developing, individual Muslims are entitled to protection against defamation, including as defamation as Muslims. . . . But that does not mean that the law should aim to protect the founders of the religion, or the reputation of God as Muslims understand Him, or the creedal beliefs of the group. The civic dignity of the members of a group stands separately from the status of their beliefs, however offensive an attack upon the Prophet or even upon the Koran may seem.

See Waldron, "Dignity and defamation," 1612–13. While I largely agree with Waldron in principle, it is a separate matter whether group defamation statutes are *being used* in such a way as to apply to speech about sacred entities themselves.

59 This was the reasoning relied upon by the US Supreme Court to uphold a group libel law in the 1952 case of Beauharnais v. Illinois, which has since fallen into disrepute among many constitutional scholars.

60 Heyman, "Hate speech, public discourse," 172.

61 Jeremy Waldron characterizes these reputational attacks of group defamation as "assaults upon the *dignity* of the persons affected— *dignity*, in the sense of these persons' basic social standing, of the basis of their recognition as social equals, and of their status as bearers of human rights and constitutional entitlements. . . . Philosophically we may say that dignity is inherent in the human person—and so it is. . . . But as a social and legal status, dignity has to be nourished and maintained by society and the law . . . ." (Dignity and defamation, 1611–12).

62 Mackinnon, *Women's lives, men's laws*, 321. "Discrimination law begins with an assumption of human status and focuses on deviations in treatment from that standard. If a man chains his dog in his backyard, only a few people would say that that dog's civil rights are violated. If a man chains a woman in his basement, more will. It does not matter if he loves or hates her. What matters is how he treats her and what that treatment and its permissibility say about what a woman socially is" (320).

63 See Post, "Racist speech, democracy, and the First Amendment," 293–300.

64 C. Edwin Baker, "Autonomy and hate speech," 155.

65 United Nations, General Comment No. 34, para. 48. See also United Nations, "Report of the Special Rapporteur on the promotion and protection"; Cherry and Brown, *Speaking freely about religion*.

66 See Dacey and Koproske, "Against religious freedom"; Eisgruber and Sager, *Religious freedom and the constitution*; Nussbaum, *Liberty of conscience*; Sullivan, *The impossibility of religious freedom*. As the Human Rights Committee has interpreted ICCPR Article 18, it "protects theistic, non-theistic and atheistic beliefs, as well as the right not to profess any religion or belief." The terms "belief" and "religion" are construed broadly so that the article is "not limited in its application to traditional religions or to religions and beliefs with institutional characteristics or practices analogous to those of traditional religions." United Nations, General Comment No. 22, para. 2.

67 Handyside v. United Kingdom, para. 49.

68 Erbakan v. Turkey, para. 68. In the original: "*un risque actuel*" and "*un danger imminent pour la société*."

69 Faurisson v. France, para. 9.6; Ross v. Canada, para 4.6.

70 Perhaps the most troublesome concept in the international standard is "hostility" since an attitude of hostility is neither lawless nor a violation of any person's rights. Even the human rights organization Article 19: Global Campaign for Freedom of Expression appears to accept this concept without reservations. Its "Camden Principles on equality and freedom of expression" define *hatred* and *hostility* as "intense and irrational emotions of opprobrium, enmity and detestation towards the

target group," and *incitement* as "statements about national, racial or religious groups which create an imminent risk of discrimination, hostility or violence against persons belonging to those groups." There are two problems with this analysis. First, if hostility is an intense and irrational emotion of opprobrium, enmity and detestation, and hatred is likewise an intense and irrational emotion of opprobrium, enmity and detestation, then "advocacy of hatred that constitutes incitement to hostility" would be redundant, and hostility would not itself generate any criminality that is not generated by hatred itself. Thus, the analysis begs the question against those who deny the criminality of hate speech. If, contrary to the above definition, hostility is something more than hatred, it remains to be demonstrated that it is a rights violation or otherwise a crime. Unless this can be demonstrated, an imminent risk of hostility should not be considered an imminent risk of illegal activity.

71 See Donnelly, *Universal human rights*, 97–8.
72 Benvenisti, "Margin of Appreciation," 847.
73 Ibid., 844.

Chapter 5

1   al-Kalbi, *The book of idols*, 28.
2   Ibid., 14.
3   Ibid., 27.
4   King, "The paintings," 223, 224.
5   These categories are examined in Habertal and Margalit, "Idolatry and Representation."
6   Ibid., 20.
7   King, "Islam, iconoclasm," 269.
8   Ibid., 274.
9   King, "The Paintings," 220.
10 Flood, "Between Cult and Culture," 647.
11 Ibid., 648; emphasis by the author.
12 Glassé, "Idols," 235.

13 See Ruthven, *Islam in the world*, 44.

14 Glassé, "Shirk," 491.

15 Grabar and Natif, "The story of portraits." Shiite portraits of Muhammad are not uncommon in Iranian markets even today. See Rosen, *Varieties of Muslim experience*, 107; Hussain, *Images of Muhammad*.

16 The extent to which human jealousy and fidelity serve as models for idolatry is explored in Habertal and Margalit, *Idolatry*.

17 Discussed in Flood, "Between Cult and Culture," 645.

18 Martin, Woodward and Atmaja, *Defenders of reason in Islam*.

19 Ibid., 90.

20 Ibid., 92.

21 Wolfson, *The philosophy of the kalam*, 204.

22 Winter, *The Cambridge companion*, 48.

23 Peters, *God's created speech*, 2–3.

24 Ibid., 2.

25 At least it was relatively free for a time. Unfortunately, while they enjoyed the status of official doctrine under the Caliphate in Baghdad, the Mu'tazila initiated an inquisition, or *Mihna* in 833 CE to enforce their own understanding of orthodoxy. See ibid., 5.

26 Aslan, *No god but God*, 159.

27 See Abu Zayd, *Voice of an exile*; Warraq, *The origins of the Koran*; Warraq, *What the Koran really says*.

28 Korpe, *Shoot the singer!*, 135.

29 Snir, *Religion, mysticism*, 153.

30 Ibid., 52.

31 Korpe, *Shoot the singer!*, 137–8.

32 Ibid., 135.

33 There is a perfectly legitimate use of "sacred" as an adjective that means something like "religious," as in "sacred music." This is not the use of "sacred" that I am trying to understand. Obviously this notion of sacredness will be derivative of a notion of religion. What I am trying to understand is the notion of something important, inviolable, and incomparable, and this is typically thought to be a constituent of religion, if not coextensive with it, as in Durkheim's analysis.

34 Durkheim, *The elementary forms*, 62.

35 See Evans, "The sacred."

36 This conception of the sacred, owing mostly to the work of Rudolf Otto and Mircea Eliade, dominated comparative religion for generations. It stressed the metaphysical dimension, the encounter with a transcendent or supernatural reality. In Otto's phrase, the sacred is *ganz andere*, completely or wholly other. It is "the manifestation of something of a wholly different order, a reality that does not belong to our world, in objects that are an integral part of our national 'profane' world," in the formulation by Eliade in *The sacred and the profane*, 11. The notion of sacred homologies is explored at length by Eliade (166–80).

37 Leuba, "Sociology and psychology," 326.

38 Durkheim, *The elementary forms*.

39 Berger, *The sacred canopy*. See also Paden, "Sacrality as integrity."

40 Dworkin, *Life's dominion*.

41 Crosby, *Personalist papers*.

42 I do not want to commit to the claim that the reasons of the sacred must be intrinsic in the sense of being grounded only by the intrinsic properties of the sacred. It could be that part of the reason-giving force of a sacred object comes from its relational properties, as the value of a mythic *axis mundi* lies in part in its relation to those for whom it supplies a cosmological center.

43 Goyal, *Connections*, 16–18.

44 In the *Iliad*, Agamemnon invokes Helios in his oath with the Trojans (3.277). Discussed in Kitts, *Sanctified violence in Homeric society*, 96.

45 Whether and where one thinks there are qualitative differences between *moral* reasons as opposed to reasons of rationality or prudence will depend on one's view on the scope of morality. Thinkers of a contractualist or contractarian bent will say that morality only concerns obligations that persons have to one another. Consequentialists will say that morality concerns the promotion of whatever goods there may be in the world, such as the well-being of humans and other animals. Kantians will maintain that in some sense the moral domain includes any and all of our reasons for action since the proper exercise of our faculty of practical rationality itself commits us to compliance with the moral law. But

whatever one's views, if there are any moral reasons at all, then the centrality of the sacred ensures that some of them will intersect it.

46 Carruthers, Laurence, and Stich, *Culture and cognition*; Carruthers,
Laurence, and Stich, *Foundations and the future*; Douglas, *Purity and
danger*.

47 Raz, *The morality of freedom*, 350.

48 Tetlock, Kristel, Elson, Green, and Lerner, "The psychology of the
unthinkable"; Taves, *Religious experience reconsidered*.

49 Taves, ibid., 32.

50 Plato, *The symposium*, 61 (221c).

51 Ibid., 49. For a critique of the Platonic view, see Nussbaum's discussion
in *The fragility of goodness*, 165–99.

52 Crosby, *Personalist papers,* 17.

53 Ibid., 12, n10.

54 I am ignoring for the moment the additional layer of social meaning
overlaid onto the cow by the explosive politics of Hindu–Muslim relations in India.

55 Hawley, "Thief of Butter," 214.

56 From the liturgical hymn Yigdal ("May he be magnified"). See Neusner,
The way of Torah, 158. I do not mean to endorse the coherence of the
thought that God is a person, let alone the likelihood that it is true.
Arguably, a perfect being could not be a person insofar as a perfect
being would not be free and morally responsible for its actions. On
this, see Rowe, *Can God be free?* I only wish to show that if the divine
person is sacred, it is sacred for the same kind of reasons that non-
divine persons are sacred.

57 In "Moral horror and the sacred," John Merrihew Adams identifies the
violation of the sacred with the assault on essential personhood, and
personhood with the "image of God." But it is an open question which
of these is normatively prior: the supernatural personhood of God or
personhood as such. As I understand this usage of the Image of God
Thesis, it asserts that our worth is explained by the fact that we are
made in God's image, *in the sense that, like God, we are persons*, not in
the sense that, like God, we are supernatural. If only supernatural (transcendent, timeless, omnipresent, etc.) persons have worth, then being

a (natural) person would not be sufficient for having worth, and the Image of God Thesis would be false. But if personhood as such is sufficient for moral worth, then it is sufficient to explain the moral worth of God's personhood. So, either the Image of God Thesis is false, or God's worth as a person is a function of his personhood as such (God may, of course, have other sources of worth besides his personhood). The moral substance of the claim that we are created in the image of God turns out to be the claim that we are persons.

58 Those who would prefer to restrict the domain of the "sacred" to the domain of the supernatural or transcendent may object that talk of reasons and inherent worth is anything but naturalistic. Of course, this depends on how one views the nature of normative statements, moral and otherwise. There is a respectable philosophical tradition—metaethical naturalism—holding that normative statements express beliefs about what are ultimately natural facts, as well as others—expressivism, and other forms of non-cognitivism—holding that they are not expressions of beliefs about facts at all, natural or otherwise, but rather expressions of other kinds of attitudes, such as approving, accepting, or recommending. Either way, normative claims are not claims about non-natural facts. But let it be granted that normative statements do express beliefs, and that these beliefs are identical with or not "reducible" to beliefs about natural facts, that the space of reasons cannot be contained by the space of facts. It does not follow that the space of reasons is "supernatural" in the strong sense of an order of reality that transcends the physical universe and yet casually interacts with it. One could be a non-naturalist about the normative without being a supernaturalist about the sacred.

59 Consider the Principle of Total Evidence. According to one influential view of rationality, in deciding whether a claim is true, a rational person will form an estimate of its probability in light of all of the evidence available to him, and he will adjust that estimate conditional on new evidence if and when it comes to light. Perhaps practical rationality requires that when making up our minds about what to do, we ought to observe the Principle of Total Evidence. If there is evidence of the sacred—or any other

kind of warrant for believing it—a rational person will update his belief accordingly. This presents the question of what lengths one should go to in seeking evidence that is "available." A search for evidence of unknown unknowns would impose opportunity costs: other goods are sacrificed in the time, attention, and resources expended on that search. And then there is the problem of knowing when to stop looking. Perhaps the reasonable strategy is to take no steps that would *preclude one from discovering* what sacredness there may be to discover. If so, then a secular person who rejects every particular traditional story about the sacred nevertheless may have a general reason not to reject its very possibility, but rather to cultivate an attitude of openness or responsiveness to the sacred.

60 Coetzee, *Elizabeth Costello*, 65. The character of Costello first appeared in a lecture-within-a-lecture by Coetzee for the University Center for Human Values at Princeton University. See Coetzee, *The lives of animals*.

61 Coetzee, *Elizabeth Costello*, 94.

62 Ibid., 65.

63 Following the Rushdie Affair, Richard Webster argued that Rushdie's liberal defenders displayed a dogmatic arrogance that he traced to the militant Protestant belief in the inner light of conscience. He painted the controversy, therefore, as a clash of religious fundamentalisms. See Webster, *A brief history of blasphemy*.

64 James, *The varieties of religious experience*, 38.

65 1 Corinthians 4:10, cited in the discussion of "holy folly" in Berger, *Redeeming laughter*, 188.

66 Ibid., 190.

67 1 Corinthians 1:23–8, in ibid., 189.

68 Gilhus, *Laughing gods, weeping virgins*, 36–7.

69 As Thomas Nagel has observed in his essay "The absurd," the occasional impression that our deepest pursuits somehow lack metaphysical heft might be explained by a simple fact about persons, that we are capable of seeing our lives at once from the subjective point of view and from the objective point of view. From the subjective

point of view, the view from the inside as it were, our concerns strike us as real and important; they are always splashed across our psychic foreground. But our cognitive equipment also permits us to regard ourselves and our lives as objects, and in this view our concerns disappear into the uniform grain of the physical cosmos. When these two frames of reference collide, the effect is absurdity. See Nagel, *Mortal questions*.

70 Huizinga, *Homo ludens*. For discussion, see Neu, *Sticks and stones*, chapter 3.

71 Direct quotations from the Homeric Hymn to Hermes are from Homer, Andrew Long, trans., *The Homeric Hymns*, 137–65.

72 Nietzsche, *The gay science*, 8.

Postscript

1 Copland, "What to do about cows?," 60.

2 Thursby, *Hindu–Muslim relations in British India* 82.

3 Ibid., 76.

4 Copland, "What to do about cows?," 59.

5 Thursby, *Hindu–Muslim relations in British India*, 77.

6 Bratman, *Intentions, plans and practical reason*. I borrow my formulation from Hills, "Intentions, foreseen consequences," 260.

7 Chan, "Intention and responsibility," 405.

8 A consequentialist could also say that we should apportion moral blame in whatever way has the best consequences; that is, whatever leads to more well-being or less suffering. In principle, it could be best from a consequentialist point of view that we adopt some form of the Doctrine of Double Effect.

9 Nozick, *Anarchy, state, and utopia*, 74. I take from David Sobel the notion of the "seriousness" of a rights violation.

10 The classic texts on moral luck are by Bernard Williams, who coined the term in 1976, and Thomas Nagel. Their essays are reprinted in Statman, *Moral luck,* See also Martha Nussbaum's *The fragility of goodness*.

11 See Domsky, "There is no door."

12 Cohen, "The hounding of M. F. Husain."

13 Ibid.

14 Richardson, Voss, Flood, and Jones, "Disrupting the business of kidnapping," 248.

15 A related second-order rationale was invoked by Flemming Rose, publisher of the Danish cartoons of the Prophet Muhammad, in an interview after the controversy: "If one person stands up against the repression, the fear of breaking a taboo rests on that person, but if five hundred stand up, the fear is diluted and reprisals are made more difficult." In Klausen, *The cartoons that shook the world*, 19. See also Rose's *Tavshedens tyranni* (Tyranny of silence) and Malik, *From fatwa to jihad.*

16 "Terrorism is the oxygen of terrorism," says the anthropologist Scott Atran in *Talking to the enemy*, 273–9, a book based on Atran's interviews with jihadists and former jihadists.

17 The writer Taslima Nasrin, who fled Bangladesh in 1994 after facing charges of outraging religious feelings in her novel *Shame* (Lajja), experienced this in 2010 when her article critical of the *burqa* was reprinted in the Indian state of Karnataka without her permission, sparking riots that led to two deaths (Reuters, "Two killed in Shimoga").

18 Discussed in chapter 3 of Derek Parfit, *Reasons and persons*. See also Glover, "It makes no difference"; and Almeida, *Imperceptible harms and benefits.*

19 Parfit, *Reasons and persons*, 86. I am of course just scratching the surface of a vast literature in philosophy, economics, and game theory on practical reason and collective action problems. The last time I checked, there was no agreement about how to resolve the Prisoner's Dilemma, how to show that at least most of the time it is not rational to defect from cooperative schemes even though our effects on them as individuals are small. But there is agreement that we must resolve the Dilemma, and that somehow, we do.

Bibliography

Abu Zayd, Nasr Hamid with Esther R. Nelson. *Voice of an exile: Reflections on Islam* (Westport, CT: Praeger Publishers, 2004).

Adams, John Merrihew. "Moral horror and the sacred," *The Journal of Religious Ethics* vol. 23, no. 2 (Fall 1995): 201–24.

al-Kalbi, Ibn. *The book of idols*, Nabih Amin Faris, trans. (Princeton: Princeton University Press, 1952).

Almeida, Michael, ed. *Imperceptible harms and benefits* (Norwell, MA: Kluwer Academic Publishers, 2000).

Ambedkar, B. R. "The annihilation of caste," in Valerian Rodrigues, ed., *The essential writings of B. R. Ambedkar* (New York: Oxford University Press, 2002): 285–90.

An-Na'im, Abdullahi Ahmed. *Islam and the secular state: Negotiating the future of Shari'a* (Cambridge, MA: Harvard University Press, 2008).

Antonaccio, Maria. *Picturing the human: The moral thought of Iris Murdoch* (New York: Oxford University Press, 2000).

Aquinas, Thomas. *Aquinas Ethicus: or, the moral teaching of St. Thomas. A translation of the principal portions of the second part of the Summa Theologica,* with Notes by Joseph Rickaby, S. J. (London: Burns and Oates, 1892).

Article 19: The Global Campaign for Freedom of Expression. "Camden principles on freedom of expression and equality" (London: Article 19, 2009).

Asian Human Rights Commission. "*Four children and one man have been arbitrarily arrested and charged with blasphemy at the request of Muslim radicals*," (30 January 2009), www.humanrights.asia/news/ahrc-news/AHRC-STM-022-2009, accessed 19 March 2011.

Aslan, Reza. *No god but God: The origins, evolution, and future of Islam* (New York: Random House, 2005).

Associated Press. "Christian's Death in Jail Sparks Pakistan Unrest" (16 September 2009).

Atran, Scott. *In gods we trust: The evolutionary landscape of religions* (New York: Oxford University Press, 2002).

—. *Talking to the enemy: Faith, brotherhood and the (un)making of terrorists* (New York: HarperCollins, 2010).

Audi, Robert and Nicholas Wolterstorff. *Religion in the public square: The place of religious convictions in political debate* (Lanham, MD: Rowman & Littlefield, 1997).

Bagby, Laurie M. *Thomas Hobbes: Turning point for honor* (Plymouth: Lexington Books, 2009).

Baker, C. Edwin. "Autonomy and hate speech," in Hare and Weinstein, *Extreme speech and democracy*: 139–57.

BBC News World Edition. "French author denies racial hatred" (17 September, 2002). http://news.bbc.co.uk/2/hi/europe/2260922.stm; accessed 22 April 2011.

Beauharnais v. Illinois 343 US 250.

Ben Judah, Daniel. "Yigdal," in J. H. Hertz, ed., *The authorised daily prayer book* (Bloch, 1975).

Benvenisti, Eyal. "Margin of appreciation, consensus, and universal standards," *International Law and Politics* vol. 31: 847.

Berger, Peter. *The sacred canopy: Elements of a sociological theory of religion* (New York: Doubleday, 1967).

—. *Redeeming laughter: The comic dimensions of human experience* (Berlin: de Gruyter, 1997).

Berman, Harold J. *Law and revolution: The formation of the Western legal tradition* (Cambridge, MA: Harvard University Press, 1983).

Blumenthal, Uta-Renate. *The investiture controversy: Church and monarchy from the ninth to the twelfth century* (Philadelphia: University of Pennsylvania Press, 1988).

Bobbio, Noberto. *Democracy and dictatorship: The nature and limits of state power*, Peter Kennealy, trans. (Oxford: Polity, 1989).

Bowman, James. *Honor: A history* (New York: Encounter Books, 2006).

Boyer, Pascal. *Religion explained: The evolutionary origins of religious thought* (New York: Basic Books, 2002).

Brandenburg v. Ohio (1969) 395 US 444, 441.

Bratman, Michael. *Intentions, plans and practical reason* (Cambridge, MA: Harvard University Press, 1987).

Brennan, Geoffrey and Loren Lomasky. *Democracy and decision: The pure theory of electoral preference* (Cambridge: Cambridge University Press, 1993).

Byrne, Máire. *The names of God in Judaism, Christianity, and Islam: A basis for interfaith dialogue* (London: Continuum Publishing, 2011).

Cannie, Hannes and Dirk Voorhoof. "The Abuse Clause and freedom of expression in the European human rights convention: An added value for democracy and human rights protection?" *Netherlands Quarterly of Human Rights,* vol. 29, no. 1 (2011): 54–83.

Carruthers, Peter, Stephen Laurence, and Stephen Stich, eds. *Culture and cognition: The innate mind,* vol. 2 (New York: Oxford University Press, 2006).

—. *Foundations and the future: The innate mind,* vol. 3 (New York: Oxford University Press, 2007).

Chan, David K. "Intention and responsibility in double effect cases," *Ethical Theory and Moral Practice* vol. 3, no. 4 (December 2000), 405.

Chase, Anthony and Amr Hamzawy, eds. *Human rights in the Arab world: Independent voices* (Philadelphia: University of Philadelphia Press, 2008).

Chazan, Robert. *The Jews of medieval Western Christendom, 1000–1500* (Cambridge: Cambridge University Press, 2006).

Cherry, Matt and Roy Brown. *Speaking freely about religion: Religious freedom, defamation, and blasphemy* (London: International Humanist and Ethical Union, 2009), www.iheu.org/files/Speaking%20Freely%20about%20Religion.pdf; accessed 2 April 2011.

Choudhury v. United Kingdom (1991) Application No. 17439/90.

Chughtai, Ismat. "Communal violence and literature," *The Annual of Urdu Studies* vol. 15 (2000): 445–56.

Coetzee, J. M. *The lives of animals* (Princeton: Princeton University Press, 1999).

—. *Elizabeth Costello* (New York: Penguin Books, 2003).

Cohen, Nick. "The hounding of M. F. Husain," *Standpoint* (January/February 2011), www.standpointmag.co.uk/node/3646/full; accessed 12 April 2011.

Condorcet, Jean-Antoine-Nicolas de Caritat, margquis de. "Essay on the application of probability theory to plurality decision-making," in Condorcet, ed., *Foundations of social choice and political theory,* Iain McLean and Fiona Hewitt, trans. and ed. (Cheltenham: Edward Elgar Publishing, 1994).

Copland, Ian. "What to do about cows? Princely versus British approaches to a South Asian dilemma," *Bulletin of the School of Oriental and African Studies, University of London* vol. 68, no. 1 (2005): 60.

Crime and Disorder Act 1998.

Crosby, John. *Personalist papers* (Washington, DC: Catholic University of America Press, 2004).

Dacey, Austin. *The secular conscience: Why belief belongs in public life* (Amherst: Prometheus Books, 2008).

Dacey, Austin and Colin Koproske, "Against religious freedom," *Dissent* vol. 58, no. 3 (Summer 2011): 81–85.

Danchin, Peter G. "Defaming Muhammad: Dignity, harm, and incitement to religious hatred," *Duke Forum for Law & Social Change* vol. 2, no. 5 (2010): 5–38.

Darby v. Sweden (Ser. A) No. 187 (1990).

Darwall, Stephen. "Two kinds of respect," *Ethics* vol. 88, no. 1 (October 1977): 36–49.

—. *The second-person standpoint: Morality, respect, and accountability* (Cambridge, MA: Harvard University Press, 2006).

Dawar, Anil. "Teenager faces prosecution for calling Scientology 'cult'," *Guardian UK* (20 May 2008), www.guardian.co.uk/uk/2008/may/20/1; accessed 22 April 2011.

Domsky, Darren. "There is no door: Finally solving the problem of moral luck," *The Journal of Philosophy*, vol. 101, no. 9 (September 2004): 445–64.

Donnelly, Jack. *Universal human rights in theory and practice*, 2nd edn (Ithaca, NY: Cornell University Press, 2003).

Douglas, Mary. *Purity and danger: An analysis of concepts of pollution and taboo* (London: Routledge and Kegan Paul, 1966).

Durkheim, Emile. *The elementary forms of the religious life*, Joseph Ward Swain, trans. (New York: The Free Press, 1951).

Dworkin, Ronald. *Life's dominion: An argument about abortion, euthanasia, and individual freedom* (New York: Alfred A. Knopf, 1993).

—. *Sovereign virtue: The theory and practice of equality* (Cambridge, MA: Harvard University Press, 2000).

—. "Even Bigots and Holocaust deniers must have their say," *The Guardian*
(14 February 2006), www.guardian.co.uk/world/2006/feb/14/muham-
madcartoons.comment; accessed 19 April 2011.

Eisgruber, Christopher L. and Sager, Lawrence G. *Religious freedom and the
constitution* (Cambridge, MA: Harvard University Press, 2007).

El-din Hassan, Bahey, ed. *Religions and freedom of expression: The predicament of freedom in different societies* (Cairo: Cairo Institute for Human
Rights Studies, 2007), www.cihrs.org/English/NewsSystem/Articles/64.
aspx; accessed 28 April 2011.

Eliade, Mircea. *The sacred and the profane: The nature of religion*, Willard R.
Trask, trans. (New York: Harcourt, Inc., 1987).

Erbakan v. Turkey (6 July 2006) Application No. 59405/00.

European Commission for Democracy through Law. *Blasphemy, insult and
hatred: Finding answers in a democratic society* (Strasbourg: Council of
Europe Publishing, 2010).

Evans, Matthew T. "The sacred: Differentiating, clarifying and extending
concepts," *Review of Religious Research* vol. 45, no. 1 (September 2003):
32–47.

Faurisson v. France (8 November 1996) Communication No. 550/1993.

Feinberg, Joel. "The nature and value of rights," *Journal of Value Inquiry*
vol. 4 (1970): 243–57.

—. *The moral limits of the criminal law vol. II: Offence to others* (New York:
Oxford University Press, 1985): 5–6.

Flood, Finbarr Barry. "Between cult and culture: Bamiyan, Islamic iconoclasm, and the museum," *The Art Bulletin* vol. 84, no. 4 (December 2002):
641–59.

Fourest, Caroline. *La dernière utopie: Menaces sur l'universalisme* (Paris:
Éditions Grasset, 2009).

Gardels, Nathan. "Cartoon controversy is not a matter of free speech, but
civic responsibility" (interview with Tariq Ramadan), *New Perspectives
Quarterly* (2 February 2006), www.digitalnpq.org/articles/global/56/02-
02-2006/tariq_ramadan; accessed 13 April 2011.

Geary, Patrick J. *Readings in medieval history, volume II: The later Middle Ages*
(Toronto: University of Toronto Press, 2010).

Gilhus, Ingvild Saelid. *Laughing gods, weeping virgins: Laughter in the history of religion* (New York: Routledge, 1997).

Glassé, Cyril, ed. *The new encyclopedia of Islam* (Lanham, MD: Rowman & Littlefield, 2008).

Glover, Johnathan. "It makes no difference whether or not I do it," *Proceedings of the Aristotelian Society* vol. 49, supp. (1975): 171–90.

Gora. *We become atheists* (Vijayawada: Atheist Centre, 1975), www.positiveatheism.org/india/gora01.htm; accessed 23 March 2011.

Goyal, Sanjeev. *Connections: An introduction to the economics of networks* (Princeton: Princeton University Press, 2007).

Grabar, Oleg and Mika Natif. "The story of portraits of the Prophet Muhammad," *Studia Islamica* no. 96 (2003): 19–38.

Graham, L. Bennett. "Defamation of religions: The end of pluralism?," *Emory International Law Review* vol. 23, no. 1 (2009): 69–84.

Graham, Michael F. *The blasphemies of Thomas Aikenhead: Boundaries of belief on the eve of the Enlightenment* (Edinburgh: Edinburgh University Press, 2008).

Grotius, Hugo. *The rights of war and peace*, Jean Berbeyrac, trans., Richard Tuck, ed. (Indianapolis, IN: Liberty Fund, 2005).

Habermas, Jürgen. *Moral consciousness and communicative action*, Shierry Weber Nicholsen and Christian Lenhardt, trans. (Cambridge, MA: The MIT Press, 1992).

—. Between facts and norms: Contributions to a discourse theory of law and democracy (Cambridge, MA: The MIT Press, 1996).

Habertal, Moshe and Avishai Margalit. *Idolatry*, Naomi Goldblum, trans. (Cambridge, MA: Harvard University Press, 1992).

—. "Idolatry and representation," *Anthropology and Aesthetics* No. 22 (Autumn 1992): 19–32.

Handyside v. United Kingdom (1976) 1 ECHR 737.

Hare, Ivan and James Weinstein. *Extreme speech and democracy* (New York: Oxford University Press, 2011).

Hashemi, Kamran. *Religious traditions, international human rights law and Muslim states* (Leiden: Brill, 2008).

Hawley, John Stratton. "Thief of butter, Thief of love," *History of Religions* vol. 18, no. 3 (February 1979): 203–20.

Heyman, Steven J. "Hate speech, public discourse, and the First Amendment," in Hare and Weinstein, *Extreme speech*: 158–81.

Hills, Alison. "Intentions, foreseen consequences and the Doctrine of Double," *Philosophical Studies: An International Journal for Philosophy in the Analytic Tradition* vol. 133, no. 2 (March 2007): 260.

Homer. *The Homeric Hymns*, Andrew Long, trans. (London: George Allen, 1899).

—. *The Odyssey*, Robert Fagles, trans. (New York: Penguin Classics, 1996).

Hudson, S. D. *Human character and morality: Reflections from the history of ideas* (Boston: Routledge and Kegan Paul, 1986).

Huizinga, Johan. *Homo ludens: A study of the play-element in culture* (Boston: Beacon, 1950).

Hussain, Amir. "Images of Muhammad in literature, art, and music," in Jonathan E. Brockopp, ed., *The Cambridge companion to Muhammad* (Cambridge, MA: Cambridge University Press, 2010): 274–92.

I.A. v. Turkey (2007) 45 EHRR 30.

Ignatieff, Michael. *Human rights as politics and idolatry*, Amy Gutmann, ed. (Princeton: Princeton University Press, 2001).

International Humanist and Ethical Union, the Association for World Education and the Association of World Citizens. "The Cairo Declaration and the Universality of Human Rights," UN Doc. A/HRC/7/NGO/96 (2008), para. 5.

Jaffrelot, Christophe. *Dr. Ambedkar and untouchability: Fighting the Indian caste system* (New York: Columbia University Press, 2005).

James, William. The varieties of religious experience: A study in human nature (Amherst, NY: Prometheus Books, 2002).

Jenkins, Gareth. *Political Islam in Turkey* (New York: Palgrave Macmillan, 2008).

Jersild v. Denmark (1995) 19 EHRR1.

Kant, Immanuel. "An answer to the question, What is Enlightenment?," in H. S. Reiss, ed., *Kant: Political writings* (Cambridge: Cambridge University Press, 1995): 54–60.

Keane, David. *Caste-based discrimination in international human rights law* (Burlington, VT: Ashgate Publishing Company, 2007).

King, G. R. D. "Islam, iconoclasm, and the declaration of doctrine," *Bulletin of the School of Oriental and African Studies, University of London* vol. 48, no. 2 (1985): 219–29.

—. "The paintings of the pre-Islamic Ka'ba," *Muqarnas Vol 21, Essays in Honor of J. M. Rogers* (2004).

Kitts, Margo. *Sanctified violence in Homeric society: Oath-making rituals and narratives in the Iliad* (Cambridge: Cambridge University Press, 2005).

Klausen, Jytte. *The cartoons that shook the world* (New Haven, CT: Yale University Press, 2009).

Kokkinakis v. Greece (1993) 17 EHRR 397.

Korpe, Marie, ed. *Shoot the singer! Music censorship today* (London: Zed Books, 2004).

Korsgaard, Christine. *The constitution of agency* (New York: Oxford University Press, 2008).

Lawton, David A. *Blasphemy* (Philadelphia: University of Pennsylvania Press, 1993).

Leuba, James H. "Sociology and psychology: The conception of religion and magic and the place of psychology in sociological studies: A discussion of the views of Durkheim and of Hubert and Mauss," *American Journal of Sociology* vol. 19, no. 3 (1913): 323–42.

Levy, Leonard Williams. *Blasphemy: Verbal offence against the sacred, from Moses to Salman Rushdie* (New York: Knopf, 1993).

Lewis, Bernard. *Islam and the West* (New York: Oxford University Press, 1993).

Mackinnon, Catharine. *Women's lives, men's laws* (Cambridge, MA: Harvard University Press, 2007).

Malik, Kenan. *From fatwa to jihad: The Rushdie Affair and its legacy* (London: Atlantic Books, 2009).

Marcus, Jacob Rader, ed. *The Jew in the medieval world: A source book: 315–1791* (Cincinnati, OH: Hebrew Union College, 1990).

Margalit, Avishai. *The decent society* (Cambridge, MA: Harvard University Press, 1996).

Marsh, Joss. *Word crimes: Blasphemy, culture, and literature in nineteenth-century England* (Chicago: University of Chicago Press, 1998).

Martin, Richard, Mark Woodward, and Dwi Atmaja. *Defenders of reason in Islam: Mu'tazilism from Medieval school to modern symbol* (Oxford: Oneworld, 1997).

Masefield, G. B. "Crops and livestock," in Michael Moïssey Postan and H. J. Habakkuk, eds, *Cambridge economic history of Europe vol IV: The economy of expanding Europe in the 16th and 17th centuries* (Cambridge: Cambridge University Press, 1967): 275–301.

Mayer, Ann Elizabeth. *Islam and human rights: Tradition and politics*, 4th edn (Boulder: Westview Press, 2007).

Mbongo, Pascal. "Hate speech, extreme speech, and collective defamation in French law," in Hare and Weinstein, *Extreme speech*: 221–36.

Meiklejohn, Alexander. *Free speech and its relation to self-government* (Clark: The Lawbook Exchange, Ltd., 2004).

Mill, John Stuart. "On Liberty," in Stefan Collini, ed., *On liberty and other writings* (Cambridge: Cambridge University Press 1989): 1–116.

Montagu, Ashley. *The history of swearing* (New York: The Macmillan Company, 1967).

Moore, R. I., ed. *The birth of popular heresy* (Medieval Academy of America, 1995).

Murphy v. Ireland (2004) Application No. 44179/98, 38 EHRR 212.

Nagel, Thomas. *Equality and partiality* (New York: Oxford University Press, 1991).

—. *Mortal questions* (Cambridge: Cambridge University Press, 1991).

Nash, David. *Blasphemy in the Christian world: A history* (New York: Oxford University Press, 2007).

—. "To prostitute morality, libel religion, and undermine government: Blasphemy and the strange persistence of providence in Britain since the seventeenth century," *Journal of Religious History* vol. 32, no. 4 (December 2008): 439–56.

Neu, Jerome. *Sticks and stones: The philosophy of insults* (New York: Oxford University Press, 2008).

Neusner, Jacob. *The way of Torah: An introduction to Judaism* (Belmont, CA: Wadsworth Publishing Co., 1997).

Nietzsche, Friedrich. *The gay science*, Josefine Nauckloff, trans. (Cambridge: Cambridge University Press, 2001).

Norwood v. United Kingdom (Dec 2004) 40 EHRR SE 11.1.

Nozick, Robert. *Anarchy, state, and utopia* (New York: Basic Books, 1974).

Nussbaum, Martha. *The fragility of goodness* (Cambridge: Cambridge University Press, 1986).

—. *Liberty of conscience* (New York: Basic Books, 2008).

Nye, Robert A. *Masculinity and male codes of honor in modern France* (New York: Oxford University Press, 1993).

Oliva, Javier Garcia. "The legal protection of believers and beliefs in the United Kingdom," *Ecclesiastical Law Journal* 9 (2007): 73.

Organisation of Islamic Cooperation website. www.oic-oci.org/page_detail.asp?p_id=52; accessed 22 April 2011.

Otto-Preminger-Institut v Austria (1994) 19 EHRR 34.

Otto, Rudolf. Das Heilige: Über das Irrationale in der Idee des Göttlichen und sein Verhältnis zum Rationalen (München: Verlag C. H. Beck, 1963).

Paden, William E. "Sacrality as integrity: 'Sacred order' as a model for describing religious worlds," in Thomas A. Idinopulos and Edward Yonan, eds, *The sacred and its scholars: Comparative methodologies for the study of primary religious data* (Leiden: E. J. Brill, 1996): 3–18.

Parfit, Derek. *Reasons and persons* (Oxford: Oxford University Press, 1984).

Pennington, K. "Law, legislative authority and theories of government, 1150–1300," in J. H. Burns, ed., *The Cambridge history of medieval political thought, c. 350–c. 1450* (Cambridge: Cambridge University Press, 1988): 424–53.

Peters, Edward, ed. *Heresy and authority in medieval Europe: Documents in translation* (Philadelphia: University of Pennsylvania Press, 1980).

Peters, J. R. T. M. *God's created speech* (Leiden: E. J. Brill, 1976).

Pettit, Philip and Michael Smith. "Freedom in belief and desire," *The Journal of Philosophy* vol. 93, no. 9 (September 1996): 429–49.

Plato. *The symposium*, Peter Hill, trans. (New York: Penguin Books, 2003).

Post, Robert C. "Racist speech, democracy, and the First Amendment" (1991). *Faculty Scholarship Series*. Paper 208. http://digitalcommons.law.yale.edu/fss_papers/208; accessed 22 April 2011.

—. *Constitutional domains: Democracy, community, management* (Cambridge, MA: Harvard University Press, 1995).

—. "Religion and freedom of speech: Portraits of Muhammad," *Constellations* vol. 14, no. 1 (2007): 75.

Public Order Act 1986.

Racial and Religious Hatred Act 2006.

Radan, Peter, Denise Meyerson, and Rosalind F. Crocher, eds. *Law and religion* (New York: Routledge, 2005).

Rawls, John. *Political liberalism* (New York: Columbia University Press, 1996).

Raz, Joseph. *The morality of freedom* (Oxford: Clarendon Press, 1986).

Refah Partisi and Others v. Turkey, Application Nos. 41340/98, 41342/98 and 41344/98.

Regina v. Bradlaugh (1883) 15 Cox C. C. 217, 230.

Rennie, David. "Newspapers challenge Muslims over cartoons of Mohammed," *The Telegraph* (2 February 2006), www.telegraph.co.uk/news/worldnews/europe/denmark/1509471/Newspapers-challenge-Muslims-over-cartoons-of-Mohammed.html, accessed 20 April 2011.

Reuters, "Two killed in Shimoga as newspaper sparks Muslim riots" (March 2, 2010). http://in.reuters.com/article/2010/03/02/idINIndia-46587020100302; accessed 19 April 2011.

Richardson, John, Christopher Voss, John Flood, and Jeremy Jones. "Disrupting the business of kidnapping: How kidnapping harms the world economy and how governments can thwart kidnapping organizations," in *Understanding and responding to the terrorism phenomenon* (Amsterdam: IOS Press, 2007): 243–9.

Riedweg, Christoph. *Pythagoras: His life, teaching, and influence* (Ithaca, NY: Cornell University Press, 2002).

Robinson, George. *Essential Judaism: A complete guide to beliefs, customs, and rituals* (New York: Pocket Books, 2000).

Robinson, I. S. "Church and papacy," in J. H. Burns, ed., *The Cambridge history of medieval political thought, c. 350–c. 1450* (Cambridge: Cambridge University Press, 1989).

Robinson, James Harvey, ed. *Readings in European history: A collection of extracts from the sources chosen with the purpose of illustrating the progress of culture in Western Europe since the German invasions* (Cambridge, MA: Harvard University, 1904).

Rodriques, Valerian. "Dalit-Bahujan discourse in modern India," in V. R. Mehta and Thomas Pantham, eds, *Political ideas in modern India: Thematic explorations* (London: Sage Publications, 2006): 46–72.

Rose, Flemming. *Tavshedens tyranni* (Copenhagen: JP/Politikens Forlagshus, 2010).

Rosen, Lawrence. *Varieties of Muslim experience: Encounters with Arab political and cultural life* (Chicago: University of Chicago Press, 2007).

Ross v. Canada (18 October 2000) Communication No. 736/1997.

Rousseau, Jean-Jacques. *The social contract and other later political writings*. Edited by Victor Gourevitch (Cambridge: Cambridge University Press, 1997).

Rowe, William. *Can God be free?* (New York: Oxford University Press, 2006).

Ruthven, Malise. *Islam in the world*, 3rd edn (New York: Oxford University Press, 2006).

Sandel, Michael. *Liberalism and the limits of justice* (Cambridge: Cambridge University Press, 1998).

Schacht, Joseph. *Introduction to Islamic law* (Oxford: Clarendon Press, 1964).

Schafer-Landau, Russ, ed., *Oxford studies in metaethics*, volume 6 (New York: Oxford University Press, 2011).

Sen, Amartya. *Identity and violence: The illusion of destiny* (New York: W. W. Norton, 2007).

Sher, George. *In praise of blame* (Oxford: Oxford University Press, 2006).

Shoemaker, David. "Dirty words and the Offence Principle," *Law and Philosophy* vol. 19, no. 5 (September 2000): 545–84.

Siegel, Paul. *Communication law in America* (Lanham, MD: Rowman & Littlefield Publishers, 2011).

Singh, Nagendra Kr., ed. *Ambedkar on religion* (New Delhi: Anmol Publications, 2000).

Smith, Angela M. "Responsibility for attitudes: Activity and passivity in mental life," *Ethics* vol. 115, no. 2 (January 2005): 236–71.

—. "Character, blameworthiness, and blame: Comments on George Sher's *In Praise of Blame*," *Philosophical Studies* 137 (2008).

Snir, Reuven. *Religion, mysticism and modern Arabic literature* (Wiesbaden: Harrassowitz Verlag, 2006).

Statman, Daniel, ed. *Moral luck* (Albany: State University of New York Press, 1993).

Stewart, Devin J. "Blasphemy," in Jane Dammen McAuliffe, ed., *Encyclopedia of the Quran* (Leiden: E. J. Brill, 2001): 235–6.

Stewart, Frank Henderson. *Honor* (Chicago: University of Chicago Press, 1994).

Stout, Jeffrey. *Ethics after Babel: The languages of morals and their discontents* (Princeton: Princeton University Press, 1988).

Strawson, Peter. "Freedom and resentment," Proceedings of the British Academy vol. 48 (1962); reprinted in Russ Shafer-Landau, ed., *Ethical theory: An anthology* (Oxford: Blackwell Publishing, 2007): 347–87.

Sullivan, Winnifred F. *The impossibility of religious freedom* (Princeton: Princeton University Press, 2007).

Swanson, R. N. "Literacy, heresy, history and orthodoxy: Perspectives and permutations for the later Middle Ages," in Peter Biller and Anne Hudson, eds, *Heresy and literacy, 1000–1530* (Cambridge: Cambridge University Press, 1994): 279–93.

Tahzib, Bahiyyih G. *Freedom of religion or belief: Ensuring effective international legal protection* (The Hague: Kluwer Law International, 1996).

Taves, Ann. *Religious experience reconsidered: A building-block approach to the study of religion and other special things* (Princeton: Princeton University Press, 2009).

Taylor, Charles. *Sources of the self: The making of the modern identity* (Cambridge: Cambridge University Press, 1989): 75–106.

—. "The politics of recognition," in Theo Goldberg, ed., *The politics of multiculturalism: A critical reader* (Oxford: Blackwell Publishers, 1994).

—. *A secular age* (Cambridge, MA: Harvard University Press, 2007).

Taylor, Jerome. "Atheist given Asbo for leaflet mocking Jesus," *The Independent* (24 April 2010), www.independent.co.uk/news/uk/crime/atheist-given-asbo-for-leaflets-mocking-jesus-1952985.html; accessed 22 April 2011.

Taylor, Paul M. *Freedom of religion: UN and European human rights law and practice* (Cambridge: Cambridge University Press, 2005).

Tetlock, Philip E., Orie V. Kristel, Beth S. Elson, Melanie M. Green, and Jennifer S. Lerner, "The psychology of the unthinkable: Taboo trade-offs, forbidden base rates, and heretical counterfactuals," *Journal of Personality and Social Psychology* vol. 78, no. 5 (May 2000): 853–70.

Thursby, Gene R. *Hindu–Muslim relations in British India: A study of controversy, conflict and communal movements in Northern India* (Leiden: E. J. Brill, 1975).

Tierney, Brian. *The idea of natural rights: Studies on natural rights, natural law, and church law, 1150–1625* (Grand Rapids, MI: Wm. B. Eerdmans Publishing Co., 2001).

Tripathi, Salil. *Offence: The Hindu case* (London: Seagull Books, 2009).

United Nations. "General Comment No. 22 (48)," UN Doc. CCPR/C/21/Rev.1/ Add.4 (1993).

—. Report of the Special Rapporteur on violence against women, its causes and consequences, Ms. Radhika Coomaraswamy, UN Doc. E/ CN.4/1999/68, 10 March 1999.

—. Malcolm Ross v. Canada (2000) Communication No. 736/1997 (view of 18 October 2000), UN Doc. A/56/40 vol. 2 (2001).

—. "Combating defamation of religions L.35 explanation of vote," A statement to the United Nations 3rd Committee by Ms. Sara Martins, Counsellor, Portugal on behalf of the European Union in New York City on 20 November 2007.

—. "Report of the Ad Hoc Committee on the elaboration of complementary standards on its second session," UN Doc. A/HRC/13/58.

—. "Report of the Special Rapporteur on the promotion and protection of the right to freedom of opinion and expression (Mr. Ambeyi Ligabo)," UN Doc. A/HRC/7/14, 7 March 2008.

—. "Report of the Special Rapporteur on contemporary forms of racism, racial discrimination, xenophobia and related intolerance, on combating defamation of religions (Mr Doudou Diène)," UN Doc. A/HRC/9/12, 2 September 2008.

—. "Human Rights Council Resolution A/HRC/10/L Combating defamation of religions," distributed on 17 March 2009 at the Human Rights Council, Geneva.

—. Human Rights Council Resolution A/HRC/RES/16/18 Combating intolerance, negative stereotyping and stigmatization of, and discrimination, incitement to violence and violence against, persons based on religion or belief, 24 March 2011.

Waldron, Jeremy. "2009 Oliver Wendell Holmes lectures. Dignity and defamation: The visibility of hate," *Harvard Law Review* vol. 123: 1596–1657.

Warraq, Ibn, ed. *The origins of the Koran: Classic essays on Islam's holy book* (Amherst: Prometheus Books, 1998).

—. *What the Koran really says: Language, text and commentary* (Amherst: Prometheus Books, 2002).

Webster, Richard. *A brief history of blasphemy: Liberalism, censorship, and the Satanic Verses* (Oxford: Orwell Press, 1990).

Weinstein, James. "Extreme speech, public order, and democracy: Lessons from *The Masses*," in Hare and Weinstein, *Extreme speech and democracy*: 23–61.

Welchman, Lynn and Sara Hossain. *Honour: Crimes, paradigms, and violence against women* (London: Zed Books, 2005).

Whitman, James Q. "Enforcing civility and respect: Three societies," *Yale Law Journal* vol.109.6 (April 2000): 1279.

Wilders, Geert. "Statement in court" (7 February 2011), www.geertwilders.nl/index.php?option=com_content&task=view&id=1734&Itemid=1; accessed 23 April 2011.

Williams, Bernard. *Moral luck* (Cambridge: Cambridge University Press, 1981).

Williams, Roger. *The bloudy tenent of persecution, for the cause of conscience* (Macon, GA: Mercer University Press, 2001).

Wingrove v. United Kingdom (1996) 24 EHRR 1.

Winter, T. J., ed. *The Cambridge companion to classical Islamic theology* (Cambridge: Cambridge University Press, 2008).

Wolf, Clark. "Fundamental rights, reasonable pluralism, and the moral commitments of liberalism," in Victoria Davion and Clark Wolf, eds, *The idea of a political liberalism: Essays on Rawls* (Lanham, MD: Rowman & Littlefield, 2000).

Wolfson, Harry Austryn. *The philosophy of the kalam* (Cambridge, MA: Harvard University Press, 1976).

Zelliot, Eleanor. "Religion and legitimation in the Mahar Movement," in Bardwell L. Smith, ed., *Religion and the legitimation of power in South Asia* (Leiden: E. J. Brill, 1978).

Index